Praise for

GET YOUR KID INTO THE RIGHT COLLEGE. GET THE RIGHT COLLEGE INTO YOUR KID.

"David Altshuler does what people in education do not: He tells it like it is. As the former Dean of a high school (for two decades), I look to those in our community who have and use a healthy, balanced lens. David has that lens and uses it to guide families toward options that not only address immediate needs, but those that are sometimes unforeseen by families. David is more than just a consultant; he can illuminate paths that others miss. It is a quality rarely seen in this profession—or any other for that matter."

> – *Erik Shane*, *Ph.D.*, *President*
> *Leading and Learning, Inc.*

"What a thoughtful, grounded, and refreshing contribution to the crowded bookshelf of "how to" books about college admission. Altshuler successfully challenges the conventional wisdom and leads students and parents to consider what's truly important about the college process."

> – *Bruce Hunter*, *Director of College Counseling*
> *The Webb School, Tennessee*

"Sanity and sagacity. Seldom are these two words evoked when describing the college search process, and yet David Altshuler's invitation to focus on the match between individual and institution, does both. In a time when parents and students alike are frenetically driven by the goal of getting into the most competitive, highly selective colleges, David Altshuler encourages families to hit the pause button, to breathe, and to hone in on what matters, finding not the right name, but the right environment, in which the student will flourish.

> — *Suzanne Walker Buck*, Rector
> *Chatham Hall, Virginia*

"**Get Your Kid Into The Right College. Get The Right College Into Your Kid** hits the nail on the head. Applying to college is not the end-all and be-all. With a kind tone and persuasive argument Altshuler reminds us that applying to college is part of our children's development. Our worth is not defined by where our kids go to school. Our worth is defined by the quality of our time with family. Keep your wits and your ethics about you. That's what life's about after college too. To paraphrase Altshuler, it's not the cover on the book—it's the book in the cover. With homey anecdotes and formidable reasoning Altshuler argues that we are obsessed with the right college for our kids. But it's who our kids are, and how we are with them as they embark on their journey in adulthood that should take center stage. **Get Your Kid Into The Right College. Get The Right College Into Your Kid** teaches us that education, not where it occurs, is the goal."

> — *Daniel Messinger*, Ph.D., Department of Psychology,
> *University of Miami, Florida*

"As an admission Director at a private boarding school, I keep David Altshuler's books in my office in the hope that my prospective parents will read an essay, a chapter, or the whole book. There are so many nuggets of wisdom to be gleaned from David's essays and reminders to "keep perspective" in spite of the barrage of messaging and information that is needlessly stressing-out our families. David's vignettes regarding the sheer insanity and randomness of selective college admission provide humor and perspective on a topic that can be all consuming for our students and families during a time that should be hopeful and exciting!"

    – **Chris Bartlett,** *Director of Admissions*
    Proctor Academy, Andover, New Hampshire

"As an educational and therapeutic placement consultant who has placed hundreds of students in therapeutic schools, traditional boarding schools, and residential programs, I love David's no nonsense, sensible approach. As the mother of a student applying to college, I appreciate the gracious good humor and gentle guidance. This book should be every parent's go to guide about applying to college. David offers a refreshing look at what truly matters when making college decisions. His sound advice is just what overwhelmed families need."

    – **Lucy Pritzker,** *M.S.*
    Elm Street Placements, New Jersey

"What a wonderful book! Easy to read, wise, funny, and clear. The best compliment I can offer is that I am jealous of the author's accomplishment. I would trade my book, **Admissions Matters**, for his in a second."

    – **Jon Reider,** *College Admissions Counselor*
    University School, San Francisco, CA

GET YOUR KID INTO THE RIGHT COLLEGE. GET THE RIGHT COLLEGE INTO YOUR KID.

By

David Altshuler, M.S.

Langley Press, 2017

All inquiries should be addressed to:
David Altshuler
4520 SW 62 Avenue,
Miami, FL 33155

www.DavidAltshuler.com
David@Altshulerfamily.com

Designed by Anastasia Ziemba
az@anastasiaziemba.com

ISBN-13: 978-1974311880
ISBN-10: 1974311880

ALSO BY DAVID ALTSHULER:

Raising Healthy Kids In An Unhealthy World.

Love The Kid You Get. Get The Kid You Love.

Kids Learn What They Live. Kids Live What They Learn.

Table Of Contents

INTRODUCTION

Admission to a highly selective college is the least of your concerns

H ERE'S THE PROBLEM WITH EVERY BOOK ever written on admissions to highly selective colleges. Each and every one of these well-intentioned guides indeed focuses on admission to selective colleges.

Which misses the point completely.

Because only the most shortsighted parent would suggest that being admitted to a highly selective college is an end in itself. The goal is to have a kid who does well.

Being admitted to a highly selective college should be an indication that a student is bright, motivated, and able. Being graduated from that college should be an indication that the student and the college were a good fit. Being graduated matters more than being admitted. But what if being admitted to a highly selective college (hence "HSC") were, to the contrary, indicative of the fact that the child was a grind, a grade grubber, or

1

a cheater? What if the only successful applicants to highly selective colleges had parents who did their science fair projects for them? Not saying that's the case, only pointing out that admissions isn't the point, competence as a student is. What if competition to HSCs had become so brutal and so contrary to the interests of the student that the only way to "win" the admissions game is not to play? What if HSCs have become hotbeds of stressed-out students who had sold their academic "souls" for an unattractive, meaningless prize? What if the real education is going on elsewhere?

The best book on the subject, *Admission Matters: What Students and Parents Need to Know about Getting into College* focuses on fit; most books emphasize only the madness of getting in, equating the admission process to doing sit-ups. The worst books on admissions stress falsehood as a strategy. Here's some blatantly unethical advice from a 2015 book: "Schools are always looking for male nurse candidates. Try it for a semester and if you don't like it, move out." In short, lie to the admissions committee. Write an application suggesting that you want to study a subject in which you have no interest. Communicate to your child that being admitted is more important than being honest. Ick.

The very titles of these books seem designed to stress out the unwary parent. *Secrets of an Ivy League Admissions Officer, Staying Out Of The Reject Pile And Getting Into A Top School*, and *Playing The Private College Admissions Game*, all make me nervous. And I've been dispelling misconceptions and assuaging anxieties for families for 30-something years. Perhaps a book that tells the simple truth—that where you go is less important than who you are—won't be popular; sober truth seldom is.

I have a shelf full of books screeching about how to be admitted to highly competitive colleges. I don't have any books admitting that the very process is detrimental: both being the kind of student who has a chance and the application process itself are harmful to students and families. Counselors and authors everywhere write screeds about "the most competitive academic courses that your high school has to offer" and "long range, meaningful extra-curricular activities". No one talks about the developmental needs of students.

Don't misunderstand. I "get" the craziness enveloping the process. Consider another book title: *Playing the Private College Admissions Game: The Indispensable Insider's Guide to Getting Into the Most Se-*

lective Schools. The agenda is clear. Getting into the most selective schools is, well, "indispensable". No wonder parents are going nuts. And *Playing the Private College Admissions Game* was published in 1986. In the intervening three decades the madness has only escalated exponentially. Cheating in class, prevaricating on applications, and devoting your life in the service of admissions has only gotten worse. When I started my practice 30-something years ago, students who got rejected from their first choice, highly selective schools talked about having a drink. Today when students are denied at their first choice, highly selective school, they talk about suicide.

In the pages that follow, loving parents will come to understand that admission to HSCs is the least of your family's issues. Your family will know exactly what you can do to preserve the likelihood that your child can obtain the abilities to have a fulfilled and content life—at the college that is the appropriate fit.

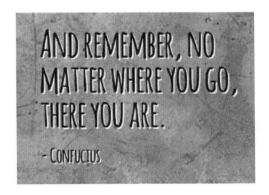

AND REMEMBER, NO MATTER WHERE YOU GO, THERE YOU ARE.
- CONFUCIUS

DON'T GO NAKED TO THE ADMISSIONS INTERVIEW

What your child wears to the admission interview makes absolutely no difference.

SOMEBODY IN NEW YORK (NO SURPRISE there) charges $15,000 to tell high school seniors what to wear to college admissions interviews.

This somebody routinely gets a roomful of misguided parents and their stressed-to-the-point-of-snapping adolescent children to pay a pile of money for advice that can be summarized as "oxfords not brogues." Or, stated less eloquently, "Don't go naked to the admissions interview." Not sure what else there is to talk about. Maybe, "A pressed pair of khakis might be nice."

What more is there to be said? All conversation about designer labels, monogrammed shirts, and the height of heels is a complete, utter, and expensive waste of time. As we'll see, admissions interviewers are next to powerless is the process of admissions decisions. But consider the implications. There are families who will pay half a semester's tuition for the appearance of an advantage.

Can you imagine that wearing a white shirt rather than a blue shirt could make ANY DIFFERENCE WHATSOEVER in the ultimate decision at a highly selective college? "We wanted to admit Percival to

Harvard. But he wore the wrong color shirt to the interview." Words never spoken by anyone anywhere.

If the competition for slots at Highly Competitive Colleges is—there's no polite way to put this—thoroughly insane, isn't it time to consider whether or not the game you're playing makes any sense? Whether or not the rules are unfair is another conversation. We're talking about whether or not it makes sense to play when the very act of participating is damaging to your child.

Imagine a distance biking event in which the other competitors are not only blood doping but also ingesting human growth hormones, EPO, and steroids. Oh, wait. Consumption of these harmful substances defines every cycling contest for a generation. If the only way to win is to damage your body, acknowledge that you're a cheater, and give up any semblance of a balanced life, shouldn't you consider taking a walk as an alternative? The cardiovascular benefits of going for a pleasant hike with family are similar to those obtained by chasing a yellow jersey for three weeks up and down the mountains. And unlike a Sunday afternoon perambulation which everyone can do, winning the Tour de France is limited to one participant. Better, healthier odds are available elsewhere. Pretty much everywhere elsewhere. It's time to reframe the question for admissions. Rather than thinking, "How do I have to destroy my life in order to have a vanishingly small chance of being admitted to a Highly Selective College?" the questions for students transform into the following: "Where do I belong?" "How can I develop actual skills rather than just the appearance of ability?" "How can I get an extraordinary education without hurtling down the road to nowhere?"

If these questions are of interest, then this book is for you.

Chapter 1

WANNA PLAY AGAIN?

> *Who you are matters more*
> *than where you go.*

HERE IS A SUMMARY OF A CONVERSATION I have been having with students and families for over three decades. I hope you'll be willing to play along too.

Me: Thank you for coming in. How may I be of help?

High School Junior: I want to go to a good college.

Me: Understood. May I ask you a few questions to make a point about good colleges?

High School Junior: Of course.

Me: Have you ever heard of Grinnell College?

High School Junior: No.

Me: You're sure? Grinnell is a liberal arts school in Iowa.

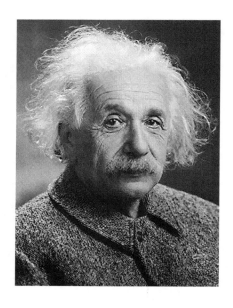

High School Junior: No. Never heard of it. I'm sure.

Me: Have you ever heard of Robert Noyce?

High School Junior: Nope. Never heard of him either.

Me: Have you ever heard of Intel?

High School Junior: Of course I've heard of Intel. They make the processors in pretty much every computer on the planet. Intel is huge. Intel changed the world.

Me: Robert Noyce found himself at Grinnell College. Then he founded Intel. When Robert Noyce died, he had billions of dollars.

High School Junior: Wow.

Me: We cannot rationally argue that had Robert Noyce gone to a well known college that he would have been MORE successful. He was about as sucessful as anyone who ever lived including Napoleon.

High School Junior: Wow. So you're saying that Grinell is a good college and that I should apply there?

Me: Grinnell is a good college. I'm not sure yet whether or not you belong there. I'm just making the point that whether or not you've heard of a school is a poor indicator of the kinds of students there.

High School Junior: But I still want to go to a good college.

Me: Fair enough. Would you like to play the "Have you ever heard of" game again?

High School Junior: Sure.

Me: Have you ever heard of Juniata College?

High School Junior: No. I can't even pronounce it. Juni what?

Me: Juniata. Have you ever heard of William Daniel Phillips?

High School Junior: No. Is that somebody famous?

Me: Have you ever heard of the Nobel Prize in physics?

High School Junior: Of course. The Nobel prize in physics is like the award given to the smartest person on the planet in a given year. Einstein got the Nobel prize in physics.

Me: So did William Daniel Phillips. After he went to Juniata College in Huntington, Pennsylvania. We cannot rationally argue that had Dr. Phillips gone to a school with more name recognition that he would have TWO Nobel prizes in physics.

High School Junior: Yeah, one Nobel prize in physics is already a bunch.

Me: Agreed.

High School Junior: Are you saying that who you are is more important than where you go?

Me: Yes. That's exactly what I'm saying. Who you are is more important than where you go.

Chapter 2

WHAT NEVER HAPPENS

Red is not the opposite of blue.
Amherst is not the opposite of Colby.

CONSIDER JOHN. AS A SENIOR IN HIGH school he took algebra II, English, and government, none at the advanced level. His electives include "Rock Music," "Evolution of the Corduroy Suit," "Weight Training," and "Office Aid"

("Thank you for contacting Schmendrick High; how may I direct your call?") His grade point average is a low B, his test results below the national average. He has no significant extracurricular activities, participation in sports, or leadership. In his spare time he enjoys watching movies and playing video games. His recommendations, like his essays, are unexceptional.

If John were to be admitted to Amherst—he won't be; mortgage the farm—he would not be predicted to be successful in the classroom where the overwhelming majority of his peers will have gotten top marks in advanced placement courses throughout high school. Most first year Amherst students have already successfully completed a year of calculus before going to Massachusetts. What math course will John take with only a background in algebra II?

There are no courses at Amherst in which he can thrive. There are no other courses in any departments for which he has the requisite background and skills.

John's failure to be graduated from a "top" college is not what is holding him back from achieving a PhD in philosophy from Princeton. John's path diverged much earlier. That John can't do well at Amherst is the sticky bit. It's not that he can't get in; it's that he can't get out.

Consider another student, this one who does have the course work, the background, and the profile to be admitted to Amherst. But isn't. (Stuff happens). Percy took five advanced placement courses as a senior, is captain and leading scorer on the lacrosse team, has 97th percentile SAT scores. His essays and his recommendations are both brilliant.

Here's what never happens: Percy is rejected from Amherst and, as a result, doesn't go to a four-year college at all. Instead, he enrolls at the local community college, studies automotive repair, is unable to handle the curriculum, and flunks out. After drinking wine in the gutter for a number of years, he moves into a trailer with an older woman and her three children.

And then he gets a tattoo.

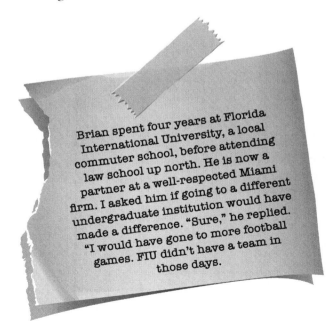

Brian spent four years at Florida International University, a local commuter school, before attending law school up north. He is now a partner at a well-respected Miami firm. I asked him if going to a different undergraduate institution would have made a difference. "Sure," he replied. "I would have gone to more football games. FIU didn't have a team in those days.

Oh, for goodness gracious sakes. Percy does nothing of the kind. You know what happens to Percy when he gets rejected from Amherst?

He goes to Colby. And then he goes to law school. And lives happily—or as happily as he would have had he matriculated at Amherst—ever after.

Colby is one of our country's great liberal arts colleges. In close to 30 years of practice, I've never sent a student there who ended up anything but blissfully happy. Maybe the average SAT scores of Amherst kids are slightly higher than those of the Colby kids. Whatever. If Percy has the profile to be admitted to Amherst and gets an unlucky roll of the dice—it happens—then he has the ability to be successful elsewhere. He goes to Colby and studies his butt off and learns a bunch and goes to grad school.

Unless of course Percy believes in "Amherst or Die." In which case, he won't go to Colby. He'll sit around feeling wronged. He'll say: "What was the point of all that studying? Why did I take all those advanced placement courses? I have to go to Colby. Oh, the horror." Here is a man who marries for money rather than for love. Here's a man who doesn't understand the joy of competition, who won't play unless he knows he can win. Hyper-focused on the future, he is unable to enjoy now.

In which case he has deeper issues, problems that Amherst is not close to capable of addressing.

As always, it's not the dog in the fight, it's the fight in the dog. Kids with skill in and out of the classroom do well long term. Kids without ability have issues that are independent of their placement. The expression, "No matter where you go, there you are" is true of our psychological baggage as well as where our children end up going to college.

What's the take away for loving parents who want what is best for their children? Focus on who your kids are, not where your kids are. Help your children acquire the skills that will allow them to be successful were they to be admitted to Amherst.

Because cream does rise to the top. Even if, as frequently occurs, Amherst happens to choose a different container.

Chapter 3

WHAT ELSE NEVER HAPPENS

The skills of the kid matter more than the location of the kid.

"**B**UT I KNOW A KID WHO WENT TO Amherst and he met this guy who knew somebody at an investment bank and now the kid makes a lot of money working at the bank and if he hadn't gone to Amherst he wouldn't have met that guy and gotten the job at the bank and the good salary." You're right.

He wouldn't have met that guy. He would have met another guy.

Good fortune may be the marriage of preparation and opportunity but that Amherst guy is going to be working his tush off. That Amherst guy has the SKILLS to GET THE JOB DONE at the investment bank or anywhere else. He has the organizational ability, the motivation, and the willingness to stay late. He knows when to say "yes, sir" and when to stand up for what he knows is right. In short, it's the fight in the kid not the kid in the fight. Here's why the Amherst kid does well no matter which introduction he gets from which guy at which bank: What do we know about the kids who have the rare combination of abilities to make a successful application to Amherst? They're smart, they work hard, have good grades. Lock one of those Amherst kids in a small closet with only a bare light bulb, a loaf of stale bread, and an organic chemistry book. A week later, the kid emerges. And can tell you all there is to know about covalent bonding because the kid has, for all intents and purposes, memorized the book.

He succeeds because he is an Amherst kid. Even if he goes to Colby.

Chapter 4

CASINO ADMISSIONS

ILL FITZSIMMONS IS THE DIRECTOR OF admissions and financial aid at Harvard. I don't know him personally, but I have heard him speak at conferences in Boston a couple of times. Here is what he said twenty years ago, back when Harvard was admitting about 20% of its applicants. Bill asked the counselors in the audience to imagine a flight of stairs with five steps. On each step were one fifth of the applications. The folders on the top step were in the "yes" pile; the folders in each of the next four steps were divided into second best, third best and so on.

Today, your kids find out by email whether or not they are admitted to a college. A generation ago, kids waited by the mailbox for a typed letter. Twenty years ago, colleges were just starting to send acceptance and rejection letters using computers: "we are pleased to offer you a space in the class or 1996" or "we regret to inform you that we had too many qualified applicants" were still the options.

So the "yes" pile is on the top step. The other four steps contain the rejected kids. But what if there were a mistake and the top two steps were swapped? What if all the kids on the top step who should have received "we are pleased" got "we regret to inform you" instead? And what if the kids on the second step who should have got "regret to inform you" got "we are pleased" instead? What if the computer messed up and all the wrong kids got in and all the "top" kids got rejected by mistake?

Bill said that no one—no professor, no teaching assistant, no coach, no librarian, no roommate, no maintenance person, no one— would ever be able to tell the difference.

Think random.

When Allie runs 26.2 miles in three hours and David runs 26.2 miles in four hours, we say with conviction that Allie is faster than David. But when Terry is admitted to Harvard and Robin is rejected, I say that Terry is "luckier" than Robin. Especially when Terry and Robin were both graduated first in their class at their respective high schools, both got a perfect score on the SAT, and were both presidents of the glee club. Terry and Robin both speak four languages fluently and both built a nuclear submarine in their respective basements. One got in and the other didn't.

Random.

Chapter 5

MORE CASINO ADMISSIONS

Each child is exceptional. Each child is qualified. How are decisions made?

HERE'S ANOTHER WAY TO UNDERSTAND the random aspect of admissions. Consider the folders of these nine applicants: Austin will be graduated first in her class of 700 kids. She scored 1600 on the new SAT, a perfect score.

Austin was president of the senior class. She took nine advanced placement courses in high school and earned a score of "five" (the highest possible) on each. Her essays and recommendations are extraordinary.

Ben was the captain of the basketball team and a standout player in water polo as well. Ben was top ten percent of his class. Ben took six advanced classes in high school and scored a "four" or a "five" on each one. Ben's essays and recommendations are extraordinary. His coaches believe he can play college ball.

19

Cassie is first generation, neither of her parents attended college. Cassie is in the top 20% of her competitive suburban high school. She scored 1300 on the SAT. Cassie takes two buses to get to school every day. Her grades would be even better except Cassie works 20 hours a week to help support her family.

Darren scored 1400 on his SAT and is in the top 20% of his class. According to the teachers, counselors, and principal, Darren basically runs the school. Darren has positions of leadership in three organizations and is president of the student council. Darren works tirelessly and effectively and is beloved by students and faculty alike.

Elena emigrated from South America when both parents were killed by terrorists. Elena has lived in a homeless shelter but has managed to be a top student at her inner city high school. Elena has only taken three advanced placement exams, every one that her high school offers. Elena's B+ grade point average places her transcript in the top 20% of the class.

Frederick has a low B average at his high school. He does not participate in extracurricular activities. He does take math courses at the local college, abstract algebra, linear algebra, advanced calculus, number theory, and topology. He has patented inventions. He has built the majority of a nuclear submarine in his basement. Of course, he has perfect scores on the SAT. In their recommendations, Frederick's mediocre grades notwithstanding, his teachers refer to him as "the brightest student they have ever taught."

Greta transferred as a junior when her diplomat parents were transferred to the states. Therefore, she will not be graduated at the top of her class. She speaks five languages at the translator level.

Harrison is fifth generation. His grandparent's grandparents were among the founders of the college; their name appears prominently on-campus buildings. His parents are extraordinarily wealthy and will likely contribute millions to the college when Harrison matriculates. Were he not to be admitted, Harrison's parents would be outraged and less generous.

Ingrid has straight As in her solid curriculum although she has only taken two advance placement courses. She might have done even better academically except that she practices the French horn three hours every day and is a paid performer of the symphony orchestra in her major city.

Richard Moll in his seminal 1979 *Playing the Private College Admissions Game* explained the above exercise more eloquently that I have. But the punch line is the same. At competitive colleges, you have to pick one folder out of the nine above.

The pressure is enormous. The professors want you to accept Austin, the student; the coaches want Ben, the athlete; the community insists that you admit Cassie, the first generation kid; the development office is pushing hard for Harrison, the development case. Every child has an advocate.

All the students are immensely well qualified. All of them will do beautifully in the classroom and out. None is predicted to be a discipline problem or have an issue with alcohol.

But you can only pick one.

And the exercise above is easy. Because today instead of picking one out of nine, you have to pick one out of 20. That's right. In the most recent admissions cycle, Stanford admitted fewer than 5% of applicants. Do the math. That's 19 "we are sorry to inform you" letters for every "we are pleased."

Selective colleges can fill their classes with valedictorians. Or students who have a perfect score on the SAT. Or captains of sports teams. Or kids who scored the winning touchdown. Or kids who were graduated first in their class AND have perfect SAT scores AND scored the winning touchdown.

Talk about random and arbitrary. A casino makes sense by comparison. There are fewer variables.

Which brings us to our first scam.

Chapter 6

FIRST SCAM

It is easier to explain who was admitted after the decisions are made.

IGH SCHOOL GUIDANCE COUNSELORS have a pronounced tendency to pretend to know which kids will get into which highly selective colleges. It goes something like this: "Oh yes, I knew Austin would be admitted. She is an extraordinary scholar after all." Or alternatively, "Of course, I'm disappointed that Ingrid was denied. But French horn players are a dime a dozen this cycle." Can you spot the swindle? The counselor is explaining what happened after the results are known. "Post hoc ergo propter hoc" as my dad, who studied logical fallacies, would say. "After this, therefore resulting from it." Here's an easier way to understand the perfidy. Imagine shooting an arrow at the side of a barn. Then grabbing a can of paint and a brush and drawing a target AROUND WHERE THE ARROW HAS ALREADY LANDED.

It's harder to hit the target when it has already been drawn. And it's harder to predict who will be admitted from the stack of nine—or twenty—folders.

Yes, we occasionally hear about a kid admitted to all eight Ivy League schools. Note that the child is likely first generation, under represented, in addition to being brilliant and, frequently, an Olympic caliber athlete as well. Of course, you also hear on occasion about someone who won money at the craps table. "My buddy George turned $10 into $2560", breathlessly explains his friend. "He rolled a seven on eight consecutive tries all while standing on his left foot and wearing a green shirt." George's extraordinary victory at the casino notwithstanding, I am not going to mortgage my house, fly to Las Vegas, and bet all my money on a roll of the dice while standing on my left foot while wearing a green shirt. Lots of people gamble and lose. And lots of kids are not admitted to highly competitive schools. Indeed, most kids aren't.

Believing that there is something better about the kid who got admitted to a highly selective college is like believing that George had some kind of control over the dice.

The absurdity of believing that George won through skill rather than luck holds up in admissions as well: if you are gambling your child's future on her acceptance to a highly selective school, you are making a desperate mistake. As we'll see, hurtling down the road to nowhere harms children and increases the likelihood that they'll end up in the wrong place. The wrong place in every sense of the phrase.

24

Chapter 7

NO MATTER WHERE YOU GO THERE YOU ARE

H ARVARD HAS A NEW ENGINEERING school. I hear it's well equipped. Let's say that Bill Fitzsimmons, the director of admission and financial aid, owes me a favor. I don't want to say too much about it but the back-story involves a life raft and a polar bear with anger management issues.[1] So let's just say that Bill wants to pay me back for my resourcefulness with the grouchy Ursus maritimus and has offered to grant me one free admit to the Harvard class of 2022 for the first year student of my choice. As it happens, I have a client who is—there's no way to put this politely—a marsupial. Specifically my client is a wallaby.

So, thanks to Bill, this wallaby moves in to the dorm, picks up a Harvard sweatshirt at the bookstore, and starts class studying physics, chemistry, calculus, and Introduction to Engineering.

---

[1] For the chronically irony impaired, I have never met Bill Fitzsimons. Although I have heard him speak at conferences a couple times, Bill does not know this author from Adam's house cat. He certainly doesn't owe me a favor.

She goes to class, studies hard, goes for extra help, sees the teaching assistants during office hours. She forms a study group with the other kids. In short she does the best she can what with being a wallaby and all, lacking opposable thumbs with which to turn the pages of the science textbooks. How well do you think the wallaby is going to do on the first exam?

I agree. She will fail all her exams. She will be put on academic probation and then be expelled for poor grades. She will be off like a prom dress, bless her heart. Her poor performance in the classroom may impact her self-esteem. Clearly, the intellectual, social, and emotional needs of Katie the wallaby would have been better served elsewhere. Possibly Princeton.

But the point remains; being admitted to the wrong school is only half the issue. Katie not only has to get in, she has to stay in; she has to not only survive but thrive. The engineering school at Harvard is the wrong place for her.

"But the example of Katie the Wallaby isn't fair. What about a kid who COULD do well at a highly selective college and gets an unlucky roll of the dice?

I thought you'd never ask. The data tell an unequivocal story. In the next chapter.

Chapter 8

EXAMPLES

*Kids do well because of who they are.
not where they are.*

KIDS WHO HAVE ABILITY DO WELL. It's because of who they are, not where they went. If you want to help your kid be successful in every meaningful sense, stop worrying about where she will go to college. Focus instead on what she is able to do. Put down the college guides and pick up a novel. Stop worrying about which extra-curriculars will "look good" on your application and go camping with your kids.

Do you think Condoleezza Rice puttered away her youth focusing on going to a highly selective college? Of course not. Instead, she became well educated. She went to the University of Denver and then went on to become the Secretary of State of the United States. Had Condoleezza Rice matriculated at Stanford University rather than the University of Denver, do you think she would have gone on to become the secretary of state of TWO countries, say the United States AND Canada?

Warren Buffet has $63 billion dollars. That's more money than the countries of Ghana and Cambodia together. Warren Buffet was undergrad at the University of Nebraska. Had he attended Harvard, do you think he would have been MORE successful as an investor? "If only I had been admitted to Harvard," he laments. "Then I would have more money than Ghana, Cambodia AND Canada." Words Warren Buffet never spoke.

Too bad Ismat Kittani attended Knox College, a wonderful liberal arts school in Illinois that admits virtually every qualified applicant. If only he had gone to Princeton. Rather than being president of the United Nations General Assembly, doubtless he would be president of the solar system instead.

I feel especially sorry for Howard Schultz. The CEO of Starbucks has a lousy 23,571 stores sprinkled across the planet. The United States is home to 5022 of them, but there are only 92 Starbucks stores in Argentina. Howard Schultz went to the University of Northern Michigan. Had he gone to a "good" school instead, surely he would have 93 Starbucks locations in Argentina.

Maybe you've heard of Martin Luther King, Jr. Had he attended Cornell University rather than Morehouse College, can you imagine that his influence and legacy would have been more profound?

Linus Pauling went to Oregon State University. Doubtless, had he gone to Stanford, he would have THREE Nobel prizes. (That's right. The graduate of Oregon State is the only person ever to have two unshared Nobel prizes. Pauling published 850 scientific papers in a career that can only be described as prodigious. Remember that a published scientific paper basically contains an idea that NO ONE HAS EVER THOUGHT OF BEFORE. Pauling came up with about one of these a month from one decade to the next.)

Joe Biden was the Vice President of the United States. Biden attended The University of Delaware. Ronald Reagan went to Eureka College in Illinois. Whatever your political persuasion, you have to allow that these two were "top of their class". Had Biden gone to a better known college, would he have been vice-president of Napoleonic Europe? Would President Reagan have been president of the Roman Empire?

And the reverse is also true. Lots of successful, content, happy people attended No Name U aka "North Cornstalk University." Similarly, you and I both know lots of folks who attended highly selective colleges who are saying "Do you want fries with that?" Being admitted to, even being graduated from, a highly selective college is no guarantee of any good outcome. As always, it's the kid in the school, not the school in the kid.

Chapter 9

NOW WHAT?

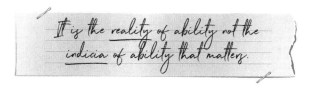

It is the reality of ability not the indicia of ability that matters.

S O IF IT DOESN'T MATTER WHERE MY KID goes to college, what does matter?

What matters is what your kid can DO, not where your kid WENT. Ultimately it's about the reality rather than

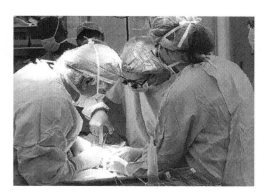

the indicia or ability. Think about the last time you got on an airplane. Did you want to know what grade the pilot got in aeronautical engineering? No, you wanted to know whether or not she had the skill to fly a plane, to make good decisions in difficult circumstances, to land a plane in the ocean if necessary. Think about the last time a family member needed an appendectomy. Did you want to know what grade the surgeon got in organic chemistry? No, you wanted to know whether or not she had the skill to remove your daughter's appendix and save her life. The ability of the pilot and the surgeon are what matters, not where they went to school.

I also work with families who have thrown out the baby with the bath water. By focusing exclusively on where the kid will go to college, they ignore the most fundamental issue of parenting, namely the  relationship between parent and child. Concentrating on what your child can DO rather than what it looks like she can do is the best way to ensure that your child will have the skills necessary to be successful AND that your child will be willing to pick out a good nursing home for you.

Imagine a home in which the conversation never deviates from the credentialing of the students. I'm not talking about a loving dad who says, "Hurry up and finish your homework so we can go to the park and toss the football." To the contrary, I am referencing a huge number of parents in this country whose only interaction with their children revolves around poking them with a metaphorical stick: "what have you done today to increase your chances of being admitted to an HSC?" Sometimes the stick is real, not just figurative. I work with many families who alter their children's brain chemistry to force the kids to study more. Again, I'm not talking about necessary and prescribed medications for attentional issues. I am pointing out the many, many families who try to confer an advantage by giving their children amphetamines. Can you think of anything—short of overt physical abuse—more likely to engender resentment on the part of children? "My mom forced me to take drugs because she wasn't satisfied with my grade in math. As a result, I am appreciative and loving" are words no child uttered ever. Kids would much rather be who they are than have their brain chemistry altered in the name of admissions to HSCs. But parents are willing to do almost anything to get a leg up on the perceived competition.

Speaking of cheating, you might be surprised what goes on in the name of getting admitted to HSCs. Read on.

Chapter 10

EVERYBODY'S CHEATING ANYWAY

If you want to raise honest kids, don't teach them to cheat in admissions.

T HAT EVERYONE ELSE IS CHEATING anyway is a poor argument for cheating. To the contrary. That everyone is cheating anyway is a good argument for redefining how to win. And as we'll see, the only way to win is not to play.

Jonathan's profile is over flowing with modest grades in English, poor verbal test scores. He has never read a book that was not assigned and has overlooked many books that were. His most articulate replies in the classroom are mono-syllabic grunts, yet Jonathan's college admissions essays are replete with "plethoras," "turpitudes," and "obdurates".

I'm thinking his highly educated, yet equally misguided, mother wrote them.

Don't misunderstand: college admissions essays are the toughest academic obstacle many 17-year-olds have faced.

Applicants feel they are being judged; they only have experienced writing compositions, not personal essays; they are not sure how—or whether—to communicate their innermost thought and feelings.

It's a tall order.

Just the same, I try to imagine the dinner table conversation in Jonathan's home: "Your father and I are sending you to college where you will take first year composition classes and write essays. But we've written your college admissions essays for you."

"Why, Mom?"

"Because where you are admitted to college is more important than what is in your head."

"Uh, OK. Pass the bottle of Chateau Mouton Rothschild, please."

But you know that bottle is just for show. The bottle is empty.

"Yeah, Mom. I know."

You've met Jonathan and his parents. We all have. They were ahead of us in line at the amusement park when Jonathan was 14. His parents were coaching him about what to say to the ticket seller. "Tell him you're 12, so your ticket will cost $35 instead of $50."

Jonathan's parents may be sowing seeds for a crop they would prefer not to harvest: their poor model of ethical behavior may have predicable consequences. Some years later—now a senior in high school—Jonathan comes home late:

"Jonathan, you were supposed to be home by eleven o'clock."

"Sorry, Mom."

"It's well after midnight. What do you have to say for yourself?"

"The traffic was terrible. I-95 was backed up for miles. A 747 made an emergency landing on the interstate. I'm sure it was on the news. Didn't you see the footage? There may have been aliens involved. There were zebras everywhere."

"Are you kidding? Aliens? Zebras? That never happened! You're lying! Where did you learn to disregard the truth like that?"

"In line at the amusement park."

"I beg your pardon? We have ethics in this family. How much is your good name worth?"

"Fifteen dollars, Mom. Same as yours."

Which is not to suggest that a stringent moral code is the only way to bring up ethical kids. And Lawrence Kohlberg would agree that there is a difference between prevaricating about age and lying about authorship. I'm only arguing that kids learn what they live and that "from apple trees, you don't get pears".

"But everybody is cheating," my college counseling clients tell me. I do not dispute this claim.

Perhaps the following example will make the point:

Monica, a 20-year-old anthropology major at a college whose name you would recognize, tells me: "My roommate goes to fraternity parties, has seven glasses of wine, and goes home with someone new every

Saturday night. She is disappointed and surprised when the young men don't call, but that's not what I wanted to ask you about. My question is about me. In my culture, we don't get drunk and have sex on the first date. Am I at a competitive disadvantage in the market place for boyfriends?"

"No, Monica," I would argue. "You are at a competitive disadvantage only for boys who drink seven glasses of wine and have sex on the first date." If you want to catch a trout, don't go fishing in a herring barrel. In the meantime, perhaps you could introduce your roommate to Jonathan.

What is there to be said about parents who write college entrance essays for their high school seniors? I have argued in my first three books: Love your children for who they are, not for what they do. I have suggested that if parents love the kids they get, that they'll get the kids they'll love. There's a line between encouraging your children to be their best selves and disparaging them for not being someone else.

Writing college admissions essays for your kids communicates that the essays they themselves have written are just not good enough—a damaging idea to communicate to a student writing a personal essay for the first time.

And for the record: my colleagues in admissions offices can smell an essay written by a parent from across the room. The "plethoras," "turpitudes," and "obdurates" give them away every time.

Before you can say, "everybody knows that, mom!" check out the independent admissions counselor who committed an act of perfidy so outrageous she was the envy of all the white-collar criminals at the swimming pool at the federal corrections agency. Ethical counseling is about helping students to find their voice, develop an idea. Good counselors show students well written essays from previous years. There are conversations about "show, don't tell" and how to communicate "hidden agendas." Effectively, good counselors teach a course in expository writing. They explain how a personal essay differs from a traditional five-paragraph theme.

Good counselors aren't afraid to say, "This essay does not represent your best work. You may wish to delete this paragraph. You might just want to start over. I know you can do better."

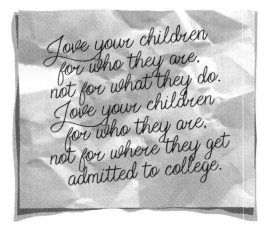

Love your children for who they are, not for what they do. Love your children for who they are, not for where they get admitted to college.

Of course another way to go about it is just to charge a ton of money and agree to write the essays for the kids. Let's call this process of "helping" kids to write their college admissions essays, "The Enron Method." Counselors writing essays for applicants is not just immoral, it's disgusting. We're sending you off to college where you will be expected to—stop me if I'm going too fast—write essays. But in order to help you be admitted to said college, we're going to hire some creep to write your admissions essays for you. Yuk.

As Graham Greene said, "when a man marries his mistress, a position becomes vacant." Similarly, when a creep commits a crime by writing an admissions essay for one student, the creep does not necessarily keep that essay secret. A creep is a creep after all.

So the creep sells the same essay to two children. Who go to the same high school.

Who are applying to the same college.

Nobody said the creep was smart. And guess what? The college could not help but notice that identical essays were submitted by two different students from the same high school. Neither student was admitted.

I am arguing against cheating. I recommend that you NOT write college admissions essays for your kids. I recommend that you NOT hire a creep to write college admissions essays for your kids. I am also recommending that you think long and hard about why you would even consider allowing your kids to cheat. Why do you feel that your kids need an unfair advantage? Do you feel there is something fundamentally wrong with your kids? As we'll see, the last thing you want to do is convey to your kids that they need help, that they need to cheat, or that cheating is okay.

Colleges and Universities that admit *more than 50%* of their applicants.

Adelphi University, NY, *72%*	University of Dallas, *85%*
Agnes Scott College, GA, *68%*	U. of Dayton, OH, *59%*
University of Alabama, AL, *51%*	U. Delaware, DE, *66%*
Albion College, MI, *61%*	Denison University, OH, *51%*
Alfred University, NY, *70%*	U. Denver, CO, *76%*
Allegheny College, PA, *72%*	DePaul University, IL, *70%*
Alma College, MI, *72%*	DePauw University, IN, *57%*
Alverno College, WI, *65%*	Drew University, NJ, *70%*
University of Arizona, AZ, *75%*	Drexel University, PA, *81%*
Arizona State University, *84%*	Earlham College, IN, *65%*
University of Arkansas, AR, *62%*	Eckerd College, FL, *76%*
College of the Atlantic, ME, *71%*	Elon University, NC, *54%*
Auburn University, AL, *82%*	Eugene Lang C., NY, *72%*
Austin College, TX, *54%*	Evergreen State C., WA, *99%*
Baylor University, TX, *55%*	Fairfield University, CT, *72%*
Beloit College, WI, *69%*	Florida Inst of Tech, FL, *62%*
Bennington College, VT, *67%*	Florida State U., FL, *55%*
Birmingham-Southern, AL, *64%*	Furman University, SC, *69%*
Butler University, IN, *69%*	George Mason U., VA, *67%*
U. California-Riverside, CA, *58%*	U. Georgia, GA, *56%*
U. California-Santa Cruz, CA, *57%*	Gonzaga U., WA, *67%*
Catholic U. of America, DC, *74%*	Goucher College, MD, *76%*
Centre College, KY, *72%*	Guilford College, NC, *62%*
Champlain College, VT, *64%*	Gustavus Adolphus, MN, *61%*
College of Charleston, SC, *78%*	Hampshire C, MA, *66%*
U. Cincinnati, OH, *76%*	Hartwick College, NY, *90%*
Clark University, MA, *54%*	U Hawaii-Manoa, HI, *78%*
Clarkson University, NY, *62%*	Hendrix College, AR, *83%*
Clemson University, SC, *53%*	Hiram College, OH, *62%*
Colorado Boulder, CO, *84%*	Hofstra University, NY, *62%*
Colorado State U., CO, *80%*	Hollins University, VA, *57%*
Cornell College, IA, *75%*	Hood College, MD, *81%*

Colleges and Universities that admit *more than 50%* of their applicants. *(continued)*

Hope College, MI, *82%*

Houghton College, NY, *94%*

College of Idaho, ID, *93%*

U.of Illinois at Urbana Champaign, IL, *59%*

Illinois Inst of Tech, IL, *51%*

Illinois Wesleyan U., IL, *60%*

Indiana University, IN, *76%*

University of Iowa, IA, *81%*

Iowa State Univ., IA, *87%*

Ithaca College, NY, *59%*

James Madison Univ., *66%*

Juniata College, PA, *74%*

Kalamazoo College, MI, *70%*

University of Kansas, KS, *91%*

Univ. of Kentucky, KY, *72%*

Knox College, IL, *68%*

Lake Forest College, IL, *55%*

Lawrence University, WI, *73%*

Lewis & Clark Univ., *67%*

Louisiana State Univ., *77%*

Loyola Maryland, MD, *60%*

Loyola Marymount U., *53%*

Loyola New Orleans, LA, *90%*

U. Maine-Orono, ME, *83%*

Manhattanville, NY, *74%*

Marlboro College, VT, *82%*

Marquette U., WI, *67%*

U. Mary Washington, VA, *77%*

U. Maryland Baltimore County, MD, *60%*

U Mass Amherst, MA, *61%*

Miami University, OH, *66%*

Michigan State U., MI, *66%*

Mills College, CA, *76%*

Millsaps College, MS, *57%*

U. Minnesota, MN, *64%*

U. Mississippi, MS, *59%*

U. Missouri, MO, *78%*

Morehouse College, GA, *67%*

Mount Holyoke C., MA, *55%*

U. Nebraska-Lincoln, NE, *70%*

New C. of Florida, FL, *60%*

U. New Hampshire, NH, *80%*

New Jersey Institute of Technology, NJ, *63%*

UNC Asheville, NC, *73%*

UNC Wilmington, NC, *59%*

NC State University, NC, *51%*

Oglethorpe Univ., GA, *79%*

Ohio State Univ. OH, *53%*

Ohio University, OH, *74%*

Ohio Wesleyan, OH, *74%*

U. of Oklahoma, OK, *81%*

U. of Oregon, OR, *75%*

Oregon State U., *78%*

U. of the Pacific, CA, *55%*

U. of Pittsburgh, PA, *53%*

Presbyterian College, SC, *66%*

Prescott College, AZ, *67%*

Principia College, IL, *79%*

Providence College, RI, *63%*

Colleges and Universities that happily*admit *more than 50%* of their applicants.

*Okay, I added "happily" but it's likely true. Not all colleges are interested in only educating children who took 11 AP classes and walk on water.

U. Puget Sound, WA, **79%**	U. Texas at Dallas, TX, **62%**
Purdue University, IN, **59%**	Texas A&M University, TX, **71%**
Quinnipiac University, CT, **66%**	Texas Tech University, TX, **66%**
Randolph College, VA, **81 %**	Truman State Univ., MO, **74%**
U. of Redlands, CA, **73%**	Ursinus College, PA, **83%**
U. of Rhode Island, RI, **76%**	University of Utah, UT, **81%**
Rhodes College, TN, **60%**	University of Vermont, VT, **73%**
Ripon College, WI, **75%**	Virginia Tech University, VA, **73%**
Rochester Inst. of Tech, NY, **58%**	Wabash College, IN, **70%**
Rollins College, FL, **57%**	Warren Wilson College, NC, **72%**
Rose-Hulman Institute, IN, **59%**	Univ. of Washington, WA, **55%**
Rutgers, NJ, **68%**	Washington College, MD, **56%**
C. of St. Benedict and St. John's University, MN, **81%**	Wells College, NY, **60%**
St. John's College, MD, **93%**	West Virginia Univ., WV, **86%**
Saint Louis University, MO, **60%**	Wheaton College, IL, **68%**
St. Mary's C. Maryland, MD, **79%**	Wheaton College, MA, **69%**
Saint Michael's C. VT, **80%**	Willamette University, OR, **81%**
St. Olaf College, MN, **51%**	Univ. of Wisconsin-Madison, **50%**
U. of San Francisco, CA, **60%**	Wittenberg University, OH, **91%**
Sarah Lawrence C., NY, **53%**	Wofford College, SC, **88%**
Seattle University, WA, **73%**	College of Wooster, OH, **59%**
Sewanee, TN, **65%**	Xavier Univ. Louisiana, LA, **66%**
U. South Carolina, SC, **65%**	
Southern Methodist U. TX, **52%**	
SUNY Albany, NY, **56%**	
SUNY Buffalo, NY, **58%**	
SUNY Geneseo, NY, **59%**	
Stetson University, **61%**	
Susquehanna Univ, PA, **78%**	
Syracuse University, NY, **53%**	
U. Tennessee Knoxville, TN, **75%**	

Data taken from the Fiske Guide to Colleges

Note 1) This author has been recommending these colleges and universities to students for generations. My students have met with as much or more success than they would have at "big name" or highly selective colleges.

Note 2) These colleges admit virtually every qualified applicant.

Note 3) The research is clear: students who were admitted to HSCs but chose other, less well known colleges, were indistinguishable by every measure from those who went to HSCs. Later in life, the kids were the same: same income, same accomplishments, same outcomes.

Chapter 11

THE NEXT STEP IN CHEATING: KIDS WITHOUT FEET

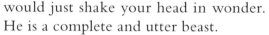

A BUDDY OF MINE IS A WORLD-CLASS distance runner. If I mentioned some of his accomplishments—running across Costa Rica, for example—you would just shake your head in wonder. He is a complete and utter beast.

Never having run more than 50 miles in a day myself, I'm in awe of someone who disdains an event of a hundred mile as "too short." It makes me tired just to think about Will running up and down 13,000 foot mountain peaks. So I was surprised when my buddy and I disagreed about cheating in running. We both love our sport. We both get chills thinking about Abebe Bikila running barefoot through Rome and winning the 1960 Olympic marathon. We both know that Hicham el Guerrouj beat Bernard Legat by twelve one-hundredths of a second to run the fastest mile in the history of the world in 1999. How could we be in complete opposition on such a fundamental issue as corruption in athletics?

Here's my position: performance-enhancing drugs, any substance that confers an unfair advantage, should be discovered and banned. It breaks my heart to train hard, run all-out, and finish fourth in my age group. If the three guys in the 60-64 year old category all took PEDs, then I'm peeved. I should be on the podium getting a medal, not the guy who conned the race.

Cheaters demean the participants and the sport.

Will disagreed.

"Broccoli is a performance enhancing substance," he said.

"What about coffee? Where do you draw the line?"

"Why not just level the playing field?" he went on. "If people want to destroy their bodies with HGH, steroids, and EPO, let 'em." Let them cut their legs off and run on blades if they think they can go faster."

It is hard to disagree with a man who can run for 36 hours without stopping or sleeping, so I will turn my attention from running to a subject about which I am supposed to be knowledgeable, admissions at competitive colleges.

Johnny has a tutor for each day of the week, one for each of his senior year advanced placement courses; Susie has hired a professional writer to craft her admissions essays; Rafa is applying to the agriculture school at Cornell even though he has no interest in agronomy; Tommy's father is putting pressure on someone he knows on the board of a competitive college where Tommy is applying.

Here's where the analogy between runners who use banned substances and students who cheat in admission becomes especially cogent: cheaters may prosper—but only in the short term. Illicit performance-enhancing drugs have significant long-term negative health consequences as well. Johnny, Susie, Rafa, and Tommy will be slammed and stressed when they are in over their heads, surrounded by more able students. They may self medicate with marijuana or pain pills to diminish their anxiety. They may be completely and utterly miserable having been admitted to colleges where they can't compete.

You think the hardest thing about Cornell is being admitted? Try preparing for a calculus test, going up against other kids who actually know the material backwards and forwards. Whether you got admitted through the College of Agriculture and Life Sciences before switching to the College of Arts and Sciences is not the issue when the exams get handed back.

The focus on winning races or admissions contests is harmful to kids. Brown and MIT admitted under 10% of their applicants this year; Harvard and Stanford under six percent. The only way to win is to just do the best you can. Play hard, play fair, accept the result with graciousness.

As the insanity surrounding competitive college admissions continues to accelerate at this family destroying pace, some parents would allow their children to cut their legs off if the child could run faster as a result. Some parents would cut the legs off their children if they thought the kids would be admitted to more competitive colleges as a result. Is deliberate amputation of limbs such a long way from cheating in the admissions process?

Wouldn't you rather have a kid who knows you love her whether or not she's admitted to an über-competitive school? Wouldn't you rather have a healthy kid attending college where she belongs, with all her limbs intact?

Chapter 12

SCAMS, PART 37
EVIL POSTCARDS
(AKA THE CHICAGO FLIER)

Increasing the number of applicants is helpful for a college; for students not so much

I T'S A SMALL STEP FROM KIDS CHEATING on their applications to colleges being creepy about admissions. Breathless students with B- averages come to me all the time clutching postcards. "Oldebrick University" wants me to apply they exclaim, eyes shining. They want me; I can't believe it. I never would have thought I could apply to such a highly competitive school.

No one could blame these kids for their enthusiasm. The postcards are brimming with enticing phrases. "Because of your sterling academic record..." "you seem like a good match for..." "we hope you will apply to..." and "you have been selected from..." abound. Doesn't an invitation to apply imply a significant likelihood of being admitted? A reasonable likelihood of being admitted? A snowball's chance of being admitted?

Not so much.

OBU does want these kids to apply. But a camel, a rhinoceros, and a pod of obese sperm whales on their way to their underwater Overeaters Anonymous meeting will pass through the eye of a needle before these kiddos from the random mailing list are admitted.

Why would an esteemed institution like Oldebrick University— Richard Moll coined the name of this representative institution in his insightful 1979 book, *Playing the Selective College Admissions Game*— want to inflate their admissions numbers? Why would they want to attract scads of fervent applicants only to crush their dreams with rejections?

Easy. As always when faced with a seemingly imponderable question, follow the money. Oldebrick University will claim that they are "sifting the coals" trying to find those undiscovered student gems. Oldebrick will screech that they are hoping to attract qualified students who might not know of their esteemed institution. (Really? There's a high school senior alive who hasn't heard of Oldebrick University and the other highly selective universities? Nah.) The cold reality is that Oldebrick qualifies for funding based on the number of applicants it attracts. Yield is the other important ratio. We'll talk more about yield in another chapter. For now, just note that rankings rely on the number of applicants and the number of applicants rejected. Rankings of colleges determine rankings with bond agencies. Bond agencies determine the cost of borrowing money to build that shiny new student union on campus. Borrowing $50 million dollars at three percent instead of four percent is real money, real money that can buy a bunch of evil post cards.

Inflating the number of applicants isn't theoretical even though the harm is personal. An esteemed institution in the Midwest changed their numbers with ease. The University of Chicago was and is a bastion of intellectual excellence. From its founding in 1890, the University of Chicago has attracted only the best and the brightest. For generations, students self selected.

Only cerebral types applied, only academic types were admitted, only brilliant kids matriculated. Do YOU want to take a test written by Milton Friedman? Neither do I. In 1971, Susan Berman explained it this way in her subversive, *The Underground Guide to the College of your Choice*, "...at other universities the professors consider you innocent of stupidity until you prove otherwise while [at the University of Chicago] you are presumed guilty of stupidity until you prove yourself innocent." And nothing has changed in the half century since the underground guide was published. UC still attracts and admits incredibly bright, intellectually curious kids. These students, unlike this author, WANT to take a class with Milton Friedman, one of the brightest guys on the planet.

So a couple generations ago, UC accepted 80% of its applicants. Everybody who applied knew what the deal was. Apply to Chicago; get accepted; listen to lectures by Milton Friedman; write 20-page papers every week on esoteric topics; study every minute of every day.

So all is right with the world. Students who didn't want to write 20-page papers every week on obscure topics applied, were admitted, and matriculated elsewhere. Everybody in education knew the deal at Chicago. The students even proudly wore a shirt emblazoned with the unofficial school motto: "The University of Chicago. Where fun goes to die."

History
Describe the history of the Papacy from its origins to the present day, concentrate specifically but not exclusively, on the social, political, economic, religious, and philosophical impact on Europe, Asia, America and Africa.
Be brief, concise and specific.

Literature
Compose an epic poem based on the events of your own life in which you see and footnote allusions from T.S. Eliot, Keats, Chaucer, Dante, Norse mythology and the Marx brothers. Critique your poem with a full discussion of its metrics.

Music
Write a piano concerto. Orchestrate it and perform it with flute and drum. You will find a piano under your seat.

Faux exam from a highly selective college. The author of this book will wait over here while you complete your work.

You have 20 minutes.

Step One: Enter the rankings. Now all is not right with the world. Because the University of Chicago admits virtually all of its applicants. The self selection of students has led the University of Chicago—arguably the most competitive institution in the country by any meaningful definition of "competitive"—to be considered "not competitive." A university admitting 80% of its applicants is not selective. And if you're not selective it costs more to borrow the money to build that new science center. The university needs to admit a smaller percentage of its applicants.

Step Two: Enter the postcards. Chicago hires a marketing firm to help them claw their way back up in the rankings. The solution? Send postcards. Send lots of postcards. Send postcards to kids who have no chance of being admitted. Send postcards to kids who would be miserable if they were admitted. Send postcards to kids who can't write 20-page papers on obscure topics. Send postcards to kids who don't understand that "we hope you'll apply" is just a marketing ploy. Send postcards to kids and turn them into cannon fodder. Instead of admitting 80% of applicants, change the promotional materials and reject 90% of applicants.

Problem solved.

In real numbers, Chicago admitted 40.3% in 2005, down to 7.6% in 2016. Eleven years ago, they admitted two kids in five. Now they admit one student out of 14. (We learned about how that one fortunate student is chosen from the 13 "we are sorry to inform you" recipients in chapter 5.)

I'm not blaming universities for getting caught up in the cold war. What choice do they have? The other highly selective schools are driving their admissions ratios down so that they can move their ranking up. The first 25 schools make the first page. No institution wants to be relegated to a subsequent page of "top liberal  arts colleges" or "top national universities" in that silly US News and World Report magazine. If a HSU admitted 10% last year they darn well better admit 9% this year. The reverse direction is intolerable. If a HSU goes from an admit ratio of 10% UP to 11% the headline will clobber them. "HSC LESS SELECTIVE than last year."

If a highly selective school is perceived by any measure as being less selective it may as well just go ahead and scrap that plan for the new 50 million dollar sports complex.

What does all this sweat and bother have to do with you and your child? What do interest rates and bonds and new science buildings have to do with your kid's admissibility to a highly selective college? Only this: a college is selective BECAUSE it wants to be able to raise money cheaply. Colleges are selective BECAUSE they admit a small percentage of the students who apply. It's the admit ratio that makes a college selective. Colleges aren't selective based on the quality of undergraduate teaching. To the contrary, at many HSCs the big name professors never condescend to have anything to do with the undergraduates. Tenured faculty don't teach first-year students; they don't have office hours for 18-year-olds; they don't interact with the younger students at all. To the contrary, full professors are doing their jobs: getting research published in erudite journals and toddling off to cure cancer and so on.

In *Colleges that Change Lives*, Lorn Pope eloquently discloses the differences between BIG private schools where professors do research and smaller liberal arts schools where professors are hired to teach. Harvard may have the best program in the country to get a PhD in philosophy. That reputation may be cold comfort to the packed classroom of undergraduates. A first-year course in economics at Harvard typically has hundreds and hundreds of students in one classroom.

Not that there's anything horribly wrong with an undergraduate education at Harvard. Only that focusing on admission to Harvard— "Preparation H" in Alfie Kohn's apt phrase—is far more bother than it's worth.

Long story short: the selectivity of a college as measured by how many applicants are rejected has little to do with the excellence of the instruction in its classrooms. If a family is more concerned for their child's education and less focused on numerical measures of selectivity, the family is more likely to find a college where the child can thrive.

Chapter 13

SCAMS, PART 89: THE MYTH OF THE INTERVIEW

I F ALL THE MISINFORMATION AND UNBEARABLE hamster wheel silliness of the admissions process to highly selective colleges, the interview stands alone. The first place prize for craziness goes to kids who spend time and treasure preparing for interviews that are meaningless in the decision making process. Alumni interviewers have no power. None whatsoever. Zilch. Nada. Zero. On-campus interviews are twice as valuable. (Two times zero is still zero.)

You know why the admissions representative often takes a picture of the kid being interviewed? So that there is some chance, however small, that she will be able to remember who the heck the kid was by the end of the day. That's right. The photo is not so admissions committees can discriminate against kids with acne. The snapshot is so the interviewer can put a file with a face. Five or ten interviews a day times several months in the admission cycle adds up to a bunch of kids. Few of whom get remembered.

An analogy will make the point regarding just how screamingly unimportant the interviews are.

How does a religious cult convince its converts to stand in the middle of a street collecting? By convincing the poor schmoe that he is a valuable part of something bigger than himself. "You're important to our church," the head zealot intones. "Now go stand on a street corner and solicit donations." Change "church" to "college" in the first sentence and "street corner" to "board room" in the second and you're beginning to understand the fund raising practice at colleges. Where do you think the billion dollar endowments come from?

Of course, I'm not comparing the brain washing and perfidy of one organization to another. Equating religious cults to the development office of a highly selective college would be unfair. To the religious devotees. The colleges are much more sophisticated in keeping their adherents adhered. After all, a guy standing in the rain selling flowers can bring in a hundred dollars on a good day. Whereas a call to a big donor can fetch millions.

A buddy of mine does alumni interviews for a highly selective school. Joanne did her undergraduate work there before getting a master's in electrical engineering and going to medical school. Joanne loves her school and is happy to "give back" by helping interview local kids. In a given admissions cycle she will dutifully meet with a few dozen kids and write up thoughtful reports. The only problem is that sometimes she can't get out of surgery and has to cancel her appointments with the bright-eyed valedictorians and nervous team captains. Understandably, she can't walk out of an operation when she is up to her elbows in somebody's intestines. So she is able to interview some kids and not others. Do you think admissions decisions are based on whether or not Joanne was able to leave the operating theater on time? Of course not.

So some applicants get interviewed and some kids don't. Do you think an HSC discriminates against a kid because Joanne was in surgery? The chances of an applicant being admitted doesn't change based on Joanne's responsibilities in the OR.

I have another dear family friend who has been doing alumni interviews ever since he was undergrad and got his PhD from a highly selective school 60 years ago. Louis can hardly be described as naïve.

He is a brilliant teacher and researcher and has written more text books than I've had hot meals. But he doesn't understand the purpose of the interviews that he gives. "I always write the applicants the best possible recommendations," he has told me over the years. "But it doesn't seem to matter. Only an insignificantly small number of the kids I interview are admitted." Bless his heart. If there is no variance then there is no score. If everybody gets a ten, it is hard to distinguish one score from another.

But Louis doesn't understand the true function of the interview. Nor does another colleague who finally gave up in frustration. He was strong for a kid whom he had interviewed. "Best kid I had spoken to in decades," he told me. "Not just brilliant but intellectually curious. Involved. A leader. Had read everything, could speak eloquently on many disciplines. Spoke five languages. Would have been a great fit for our school." When the kid wasn't admitted, he wrote to the person in charge of scheduling alumni interviews in his region. "I will no longer give interviews nor write recommendations," he emailed. "Because it is clear that you do not read them."

Ouch. But Louis for all his erudition does not understand his function in the admissions process.

The purpose of the interview isn't about distinguishing one kid from another. An interview is a yield tool.

As you remember, the yield ratio is the number of admitted kids who actually show up in the fall. If Jonny applies to eight schools and is admitted to three, there are two schools where he doesn't show up. Like popularity at a junior high dance, yield is desperately important when attracting funding. Understandably so. If none of the kids whom you admit are showing up at your college, the institution is going to shut down for want of students. Alumni interviewers are invariably successful, well-spoken advocates for their schools. If a kid IS admitted, the alumni interviewer is part of the process that helps convince him to show up in the fall.

In the interest of full fiduciary disclosure, I should admit that I feel nothing but gratitude for the extraordinary educations that my own children received at the magnificent institutions where they attended. I understand why graduates and families want to help out. Volunteering as an alumni interviewer is a great way to give back.

I understand appreciation. The fact is that if one of the schools where my kids attended asked me to host a fund-raising event I probably would.

I'm grateful. But my indebtedness doesn't change my point about the interview process.

The alumni interview can't tip the scales at an HSC. The interview is just part of the meaningless craziness surrounding admissions to HSCs. Rather than wasting time preparing for the interview, your child would be better off reading a book. I hear *Pride and Prejudice* and *Tom Jones* are still in print. I commend them to your attention.

More on what your kids could be doing rather than wasting time and treasure worrying about and preparing for interviews in the next chapter.

Chapter 14

WHAT YOUR KID COULD BE DOING INSTEAD OF OBSESSING ABOUT BEING ADMITTED TO A HSC

I N PREVIOUS GENERATIONS, THERE WAS AN understanding that studying was something done IN ADDI-TION to time spent with family. Studying and resume padding in this generation are done TO THE EXCLUSION of family time. In days gone by, "credentialing" was neither a word nor a concept. Real students learned and read, read and learned. George Bernard Shaw went to the British Museum—what the crumpet stuffers call a "library"—and read day after day. When he had read for a few years, he started writing plays that are still studied and performed a century later. Karl Marx read political philosophy and came up with ideas that changed the world. In 2017, students are more concerned with grades rather than learning. An example from 1854 and one from last week may illustrate the point.

Mrs. Lawnmower: Have you graded the homework yet?

Fourth Grade Teacher: The subtraction homework?

Mrs. Lawnmower: Yes, three-digit subtraction. Have you graded it yet?

Fourth Grade Teacher: The children turned in that homework an hour ago.

Mrs. Lawnmower: Yes, I know. Have you graded the homework yet?

Fourth Grade Teacher: No, I have been teaching.

Mrs. Lawnmower: Then, I need to get that homework back. Before you grade it. I—ahem, of course I mean "he"—made a mistake in the third problem, 731 minus 129. Can I get the homework back so that I—again, I mean 'my son'—can change his answer to the correct one?

Fourth Grade Teacher: You are aware that this is fourth grade, aren't you? Your son is ten years old.

Mrs. Lawnmower: He has to get all the arithmetic problems correct! He has to get all As! He has to go to a good college!

When the first teacher declines to allow Mrs. Lawnmower access to the homework, Mrs. Lawnmower goes on to ask to "borrow" the key to the classroom from another teacher. Mrs. Lawnmower is intent on getting the homework back so that she can make the correction.

Would you agree that this mother has lost sight of the long-term goal, that her son actually KNOWS how to subtract three-digit numbers? This mother is focused only on the appearance of ability—a perfect score on the homework—rather than the reality of ability—that her child is able to subtract. Would you also agree that this family's issues are deeper than three digit subtraction problems?

Dickens got it right 162 years ago when he parodied teachers who wanted only facts to the exclusion of any actual learning. Children in *Hard Times* didn't learn how to think, only how to recite information—information that they didn't understand. On the other hand it is possible that your child's high school courses are meaningful. It is possible that your child's high school courses help your child develop academic skills and abilities that will be useful in college. It is possible

58

> "Bitzer,' said Thomas Gradgrind. 'Your definition of a horse.' 'Quadruped. Graminivorous. Forty teeth, namely twenty-four grinders, four eye-teeth, and twelve incisive. Sheds coat in the spring; in marshy countries, sheds hoofs, too. Hoofs hard, but requiring to beshod with iron. Age known by marks in mouth.' Thus (and much more) Bitzer."

that your child's high school courses encourage your child to have a life-long love of learning.

In the sense that it is *possible* for this 61-year-old paunchy, balding author to win the Boston Marathon.

What is more likely is that your child's high school curriculum is filled with vacuous exercises with little long-term value. The reason that your children's high school teachers are insisting that the students memorize the capitals of the 50 states is a subject for another book. For now, just accept as a working hypothesis that high school teachers need to quantify their assessment. It's easier to justify to intransigent parents and administrators. "Tommy memorized 40 capitals. Eighty percent. B."

By allowing your children to focus on learning rather on the appearance of learning, you do them a great service in the long run.

As an independent admissions counselor, I ask my students to tell me about their course work. I hope to discover their passion so that I can help them find their direction. Here is a typical conversation:

Well Intentioned 11th Grade Student Who Has Been Infected with Harmful Information: I take algebra II. I have an A.

Me: What are you learning?

Well Intentioned 11th Grade Student Who Has Been Infected with Damaging Information: I have an A. Weren't you listening?

Me: I like math; I used to teach math. What are you enjoying about

59

your course?

Well Intentioned 11th Grade Student Who Has Been Infected with Terrible Information: To tell you the truth, we don't actually learn math. The teacher left. So we have a substitute. Who doesn't know math. We watch movies. If you don't misbehave you get an A.

Me: I see.

How do you think this student is going to compete when she goes to college and takes classes with students who actually do know math? How will she fare when taking the same test as other first year students who didn't have an uniformed substitute for a teacher?

The time to make sure that your kids actually know stuff rather than just having the appearance of knowing stuff is yesterday.

I also ask my students what books they have enjoyed reading. *The Great Gatsby* is a frequent reply.

"What did you like about it?" I ask. (Personally, I like Kathryn Schulz' insight that Fitzgerald has NOT written "a linguistically elegant, intellectually bold, morally acute parable of our nation" but I don't mention this criticism when chatting with high school students.) My students are seldom able to comment on any aspect of the novel other than the plot. Sometime even who did what to whom is beyond their recall. So I ask them what they read that is NOT assigned. The blank stares are deafening. My students don't read that which is not assigned. My students DON'T read for pleasure. The reason they don't read is unclear. Maybe they don't read for pleasure because they are addicted to social media. Perhaps they don't read for pleasure because they are too busy reading that which is assigned. Possibly they don't read for pleasure because they won't get a grade on unassigned books. But my guess is that they don't read for pleasure because they believe that reading that which isn't assigned won't help them be admitted to highly selective colleges.

In reality colleges are looking for proxies for ability. An A in algebra II is supposed to be indicative of actually KNOWING algebra II. In reality, colleges are interested in admitted kids who have read *The Great Gatsby* and a great deal more.

Chapter 15

A NOTE ON TEST PREP

IVEN THAT WHO YOU ARE IS INFINITELY more important than where you go, can we talk for a minute about the business or raising test scores? What about preparing for standardized tests like the SAT and ACT? Won't higher test scores increase my child's chances of being admitted to a highly competitive college?

There may be some child somewhere for whom higher SAT scores will be important in the college admissions process. For your child, the chances are that higher SAT scores won't matter at all in determining where she is admitted.

Bold statements, I know. But after 30-something years of counseling students and their families about choosing and applying to college, I think I have the standing to make a few observations.

There are some children for whom higher SAT scores will make a difference in admissions. An athlete with a 3.0 gpa needs a 620 (math plus "reading") to play college ball. The National Collegiate Athletic Association has no sense of humor when it comes to the inverse relationship between grades and scores. Eligibility to participate in sports is clearly defined. Some scholarships programs use SAT scores as a cut off as well.

But for most kids, higher SAT scores are of modest utility, maybe meaningless. Consider the following common scenario: Percival will graduate in the top five percent from his competitive suburban high school having excelled in his sophisticated academic curriculum. He will score 4s on many of his AP exams, 5s on the rest. His extra-curriculars are stellar—long range, consistent, and meaningful—his essays personable and charming. His calculus teacher, who knows Percy well, writes an eloquent recommen-

Author with his daughter, Everglades National Park, Florida

dation about Percy's ability, motivation,and thoughtfulness. "One of the brightest and nicest kids I have had the pleasure to teach in my career," she writes.

His SAT scores? 700 on the new "evidence-based reading and writing" (do you mind if we just call it "reading"?) and 760 on math. In short, Percy's scores are well into the 90th percentile.

Let's say Percy's parents hire a tutor or a series of tutors or a roomful of SAT experts or a phalanx of test prep connoisseurs. Let's say that Percy gives up reading for pleasure, camping with his family, helping out around the house, tossing a ball with his mom, dating, sleeping, and enjoying his junior year in every particular. Let's say he studies assiduously and subsequently feels closer to the 1, $\sqrt{3}$, 2 triangle than he does to his own siblings. Let's say his scores improve from his respectable 1440 to a perfect "dialing direct" 1600. ("800" is a toll free number. Get it?)

With his 1440, Percy's chances at über-competitive schools are something worse than one in ten.

With his new and improved 800 reading and 800 math, his chances are upgraded to around one in eight.

That's right. Colleges that admit fewer than 10% of their applicants routinely reject kiddos with 1600 SATs. Why? For the same reason that university professors date their graduate students: Because they can.

The tour guide at a HSC bragged about how her school rejected two out of three valedictorians. And applicants with 1600 SATs? "We could fill our entire first year class with them if we wanted to."

What to do? Given that 1600 is the top of the scale, going back to the plethora of SAT wizards and shooting for a 1700 is off the table. Given that one is the smallest natural number, graduating "better" than first in the class in not an option either. So here is some directed advice for all loving parents and their high achieving high school junior offspring: get up early on a Saturday morning; make some PBJs and fill up the canteens with lemonade. Drive to the nearest National Park and hike somewhere beautiful with your beloved

Author with his son,
Rocky Mountain
National Park, Colorado

child. Enjoy the panorama. Do not talk about admission to competitive colleges. Do not talk about how higher SAT scores improve your child's chances of admission to a psycho-competitive college from 10% to 12.5%. Subsequently, if your child is admitted to Stanford, she may consider matriculating there. I hear Palo Alto is lovely this time of year. However, if your child is not destined to be a cardinal (the "color" not the bird is the Stanford mascot) then graciously accept the offer of one of the two thousand colleges in this country who would be thrilled to have a great kid like yours. (Such lovely credentials, and did you see

The author's wife and somebody else's daughter, Snow Canyon, Utah

that glowing recommendation from the calculus teacher?) And wouldn't you want your kid to go to college with other kids who go hiking with their parents rather than a bunch of stressed out dweeb-weenies? (I'm not saying that Stanford undergrads ARE a bunch of stressed out dweeb-weenies but given the 4.79 % admit ratio, there is the potential that they COULD be.)

Take it to the bank: good kids—academically motivated, intellectually curious, pleasant students—do well WHERE EVER they go. Don't believe me? Check out the Yale Law School website listing where their first year students went undergrad. There are schools represented you have never even heard of. So there.

Time to stop reading this chapter and go plan the next day of hiking with your beloved high school student. Because whatever she gets on her SAT and wherever she goes to college, these glorious days are not going to come again.

**The author and his feet,
California.**

Chapter 16

MORE CRAZINESS

OBBES IS OFTEN REFERENCED AS having pointed out that life is "solitary, poor, nasty, brutish, and short." Less quoted but equally cheerful is his "Omni contra omni," all against all. While this is certainly one view, here's another: you are not starving; your child is not starving. Yes, we're all going to die, but probably not today and certainly not as a result of attending this college rather than that.

Competition makes sense on the football field. Some teams win, others lose each Sunday. Count on it. Competition is also an appropriate paradigm for evolution. Less so for raising a child. Your daughter is not a member of the Seattle Seahawks. Nor is she a trilobite.

Anxious parents lament that there will be competition later in life. Yes, there will be competitions over time and there will be carcinogens to which she will be exposed when she's older but that is a poor excuse for locking a four-year-old in the garage with the car running. Giving her the skills she needs to succeed subsequently depends on her having the foundation on which to build. Believing that her home is a safe place where she is accepted for who she is a good start. Allowing her to know that she is allowed to fail and will still be loved is even better.

And whatever you do, don't equate success in life with being admitted to a highly selective college.

Chapter 17

THE DOLLAR AUCTION

"THE DOLLAR AUCTION" IS THE BEST parallel for admissioin to an HSC. It's a little complicated but, I hope you'll agree, the point is well worth the work.

"The Dollar Auction game: a Paradox in Non-cooperative Behavior and Escalation" was published in the Journal of Conflict Resolution in March of 1971. Martin Shubik is the author. Here's how the dollar auction works: The auctioneer says, "I'm going to give a dollar to the highest bidder, just like a regular auction. The only difference is that both the highest bidder (like any regular auction) and the second highest bidder (unlike a regular auction) have to pay the auctioneer the value of their bid."

Mr. Smith offers an initial bid of a nickel. This bid certainly seems reasonable. Who wouldn't want to get a dollar for five cents? And, according to the rules of the dollar auction, if no one else bids, Mr. Smith will indeed get a dollar for a nickel. Not a bad deal in these tough economic times.

Ms. Jones, however, bids a dime, reasoning as follows: I can get a dollar for ten cents. That's a good deal. I'll have to pay a dime and Mr. Smith will have to pay a nickel. But I'll get a dollar for my dime and he'll get nothing for his nickel.

(For the sake of simplicity, I will limit the explanation to just Mr. Smith and Ms. Jones. The argument doesn't change with more people.)

Mr. Smith is now in a tricky spot: If he remains quiet, he loses a nickel. Ms. Jones will get the dollar, paying only a dime and he will get nothing for his nickel. Any rational person in Mr. Smith's place will bid 15 cents. Mr. Smith will still get 85 cents profit. And he certainly doesn't want to get nothing in return for his nickel. So Mr. Smith bids 15 cents.

But Ms. Jones now speaks up. She bids 20 cents. If she doesn't bid again, she will lose her dime. By bidding 20 cents, she will earn 80 cents if Mr. Smith doesn't bid again.

But of course, Mr. Smith does bid again. He has to. Otherwise he'll lose the amount of his previous bids. Similarly, Ms. Jones has to keep bidding.

Consider their reasoning as the value of the bids approaches a dollar: Ms. Jones has bid 95 cents. Mr. Smith bids a dollar. That's right. He bids a dollar to win a dollar. What choice does he have? If he doesn't bid, he loses his 90 cents and Ms. Jones wins the dollar and gets a profit of five cents.

So what will Ms. Jones do? She will do what any rational person would do. She can't lose her 95 cents and get nothing in return. She must keep bidding. She must bid $1.05. She has to bid more than a dollar to win a dollar.

Mr. Smith has to bid more than $1.05. Otherwise he'll lose his dollar and get nothing in return. He bids $1.10. Surely any reasonable person would agree it's better to pay $1.10 for a dollar than to lose $1.00 and get nothing. Losing a dime isn't as bad as losing a dollar.

Except of course that now Ms. Jones has to bid $1.15 by the same reasoning. She bids $1.15 to win the dollar.

Both Mr. Smith and Ms. Jones must now continue to bid amounts well in excess of the dollar. There is no point at which it makes sense to stop bidding. When Mr. Smith bids $4.00 to preserve his $3.90, Ms. Jones will bid $4.15 so she doesn't have to pay $4.05 and get nothing.

Clearly, the only way to "win" the dollar auction is not to pay.

The analogy to competitive college admissions is straight-forward. If your child is studying three hours each night, someone else's child is studying four hours. Should your child study five hours each night? If your child is playing two sports competitively, someone else's child is playing three sports. Should your child play four sports competitively? If your child has volunteered for five hundred hours of community service, someone else's child has volunteered for six hundred hours. Should your child volunteer for seven hundred hours? If your child is taking intravenous fluids in her arm so that she can stay awake and study, someone else's child is taking intravenous fluids in both arms. Should your child take intravenous fluids in three arms?

You see where this is going. Your child doesn't have three arms. And no child should be forced to take intravenous fluids in order to stay awake and study. Another phrase for sticking a needle in your child's arm so that she will stay awake and study is "child abuse."

The only way to "win" the competition to hyper competitive colleges is not to play.

Let me take a step back from that statement. There is nothing wrong with applying to hyper-competitive colleges; there is nothing wrong with attending hyper-competitive colleges. The problem is with your child devoting her entire life to the process of appearing to be "the best" applicant at hyper-competitive colleges. Who the child is will matter more than where she matriculates. Allowing her to have a productive, pleasant childhood devoid of the madness surrounding applying to hyper-competitive colleges is a big plus too.

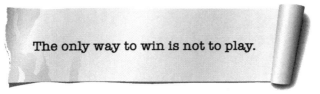

The only way to win is not to play.

71

Chapter 18

A NOT SO REAL
WORLD EXAMPLE

B EFORE MATTHEW BRODERICK WAS
Ferris Bueller and Ally Sheedy was the weird girl in "Breakfast Club," the kids starred in "War Games," an uplifting
film about global thermonuclear war and the end of all life on the
planet, that sort of thing. Spoiler alert: the world does not come to a
fiery end in the final reel. An out-of-control computer runs simula-
tions—hence the "game" in the film's title—all of which end in the
planet more or less being blown to bits no bigger than your dining room
table. Our heroes, Matt and Ally are able to "teach" the machine that
the only way to win the game is not to play. The War Operation Plan
Response learns that no strategic placement of jet fighters or aircraft
carriers will lead to one side "winning" a nuclear conflagration. Ultimately the WOPR is able to squawk in its distended computer voice,
"How about a nice game of chess?" as we stand down from Defcom
Five and our empty popcorn containers hit the trash buckets .

If a computer with an unfortunate acronym (WOPR. Really?) can
determine that thermonuclear war is not winnable, can loving parents
of high school students come to a similarly virtuous conclusion? Here

College Acceptance Rates

Brown University (Providence, RI)	9%
Claremont McKenna College (Claremont, CA)	11%
Duke University (Durham, NC)	11%
Johns Hopkins University (Baltimore, MD)	13%
Princeton University (Princeton, NJ)	7%
Rice University (Houston, TX)	16%
Stanford University (Stanford, CA)	5%
University of Pennsylvania (Philadelphia, PA)	10%
U.S. Naval Academy (Annapolis, MD)	8%
Vanderbilt University (Nashville, TN)	12%
Yale University (New Haven, CT)	7%

are the numbers. Not the arithmetic regarding how many Soviet nuclear submarines float off the coast of Vladivostok.

Seventy years ago when Warren Buffet was rejected at Harvard (big "oops", dontcha think?), the school admitted 245 out of 278 applicants from prestigious prep schools, a whopping 88%. Fast forward to the past five years: Harvard's overall admit rate has been 6.9%, 5.8%, 5.9%, 5.3%, and 5.1%. We're talking one yes for every 15 nopes.

I have written elsewhere and endlessly about the arbitrariness of selective admissions. (Chapter 4, for example.) I have pontificated in these chapters about how hard it is to predict who will be the one yep out of the stack of 15 "we wish you every success elsewhere." I have reminded my readers that valedictorian applicants with 1600 SATs who speak five languages, have patented inventions, and built nuclear submarines in their basements are routinely rejected. Today I want to help you understand how completely and utterly worthless is the whole silly process.

Because becoming that valedictorian with the 1600 SATs and patented inventions who walks on water and pees perfume can cost a kid, if not her immortal soul, then certainly her childhood. With less "perfect" credentials the odds drop off from one in 16 to significantly less. At "only" top five percent, the odds are closer to one in 50. If a kid "achieves" that academic pinnacle—first in her class—her odds at Stanford, Columbia or Princeton are still single digits. Who needs this?

Valedictorians are smart nowadays, no argument. But they also put in endless hours carrying buckets of knowledge back and forth. They learn some stuff that excites them and has meaning, but they do a ton of work that is insipid and quickly forgotten. "Top" kids are motivated, but they are also stressed and, if I may speak frankly, frequently frazzled to the point of being unpleasant to be around. There is something ungracious about the unending competition and recomputing of grade point averages.

So here's some non non-directed advice for high school students concerned about their applications to college (read: every high school student): take the AP courses that are of interest. Don't take every AP course offered just to take a shot at being graduated at the very top of your class. Develop passion and commitment outside the classroom, not a compendium of tedious community service hours. Become involved in activities that have meaning for you whether or not you think those undertakings will "look good" at Dartmouth or Rice. Read a book that isn't assigned for goodness sake. Take some time off. Go for a hike with friends. Make a minor mistake and deal with the consequences. In short, have a life. The WOPR is a machine; you, to the contrary, are a person. There's a difference. Here's some non non-directed advice for parents of high school students: focus on your child, not on admissions. If your child loves reading, if your child loves learning, if your child is motivated, if your child is content, then the future will take care of itself. Still concerned about college? I promise you that there are hundreds of colleges that accept virtually every qualified applicant and that the kids who do well at those institutions get admitted to medical school just the same as the kids who went to the single digit admit schools.

Because the only way to win is not to play.

Chapter 19

WHAT IS A DIVER'S DREAM? A NIGHT ON VERONICA LAKE

T HE FOLLOWING SATIRIC CHAPTER will make a point regarding the absurdity of obsessing about admission to HSCs.

I am determined to seduce and marry Veronica Lake. Hear me out. She is beautiful, a movie star, and has a lot of money. I just know our lives together will be exquisite. Admittedly, she doesn't know

I'm alive nor is she aware of my undying passion or my plan to be with her forever. But I know just what to do. I have been working on this strategy for the last four years and I am thoroughly convinced that it will work. I have found out the last known address for Veronica—somewhere in Beverly Hills. Although there is an eight-foot wall around the property, I have spent the last several semesters writing poetry and throwing the poems over the wall. I just feel it in my heart that she is reading and appreciating them. I also serenade her by walking back and forth along the sidewalk in front of her house singing love songs that I have written. No, I don't particularly like writing poetry nor do I have an ear or appreciation for music, but I am willing to do anything so that Veronica will notice me, fall in love with me, and marry me.

Some people have had the unmitigated temerity to suggest that Veronica and I will not be a good match, that we are ill suited for one another. These people are just jealous fools. For example, some stupid actor, Joel McCrea, refused to be in another movie with her because he said, "Life's too short for two films with Veronica Lake." And this author guy, Raymond Chandler, referred to her as "Moronica Lake." So, okay, you can't please everybody. As far as the fact that she's been married four times, well, people make mistakes. But she's so pretty. I just know we would be happy. I know that after her movie career deteriorated she lived in cheap hotels and was frequently arrested for public drunkenness, but, like I said, you can't have everything.

I am a determined guy; I always get what I want. (And when I don't, I'm not that much fun to be around.) I don't let myself get confused by the facts. I am convinced that Veronica will be impressed if I learn to play the bouzouki so I have been practicing four hours a day, all the time I can spare when I'm not writing poetry for Veronica or walking back and forth outside the address where I think she lives.

Change "Veronica Lake" in the monologue above to admission to a "top" college and you have the sad lives or many high school students. Rather than doing what gives them pleasure, they hurl themselves down the lonely road to nowhere hoping to impress unseen admissions officers at colleges about which they know nothing. Rather than taking courses they would enjoy and from which they would learn, they blindly follow dictums about what course selection and extracurriculars will "get them in."

Wouldn't this child's interests be better served by engaging in those activities in which he might excel? Shouldn't he direct his energy toward that which he enjoys rather than pursuing only that which he thinks Veronica will value? By his own admission, he doesn't like playing guitar or writing poetry and nobody likes walking back and forth in front of an empty home, yet nothing will dissuade our "Princeton or Perish" young man from "pursuing his dream," "overcoming adversity," and "achieving his goal." (Not that there's anything wrong with Princeton, mind you, but not everyone gets in.) And what about when he learns that Veronica Lake is dead? (According to Wikipedia—the source from which I got all the facts above—Lake died in 1973.) No matter how inappropriate the match, our applicant still won't give up. Wouldn't he better off following his passion, learning what he loves, and preparing himself to be successful wherever he ends up in college?

The take-away for loving parents is simple enough: encourage your children to have goals that make sense, goals that will bring them contentment—obsessing over schizophrenic, dead movie stars, no matter how beautiful—is probably not on this list.

Chapter 20

THE CREDENTIAL COLD WAR

SOMETHING OVER A HUNDRED YEARS ago, my grandmother took the subway from Brooklyn into Manhattan for her first day of work. Rachel had an eighth grade education and employment as a typist. Having been graduated from what is now called "middle school," she had a competitive advantage over the majority of folks who had no such credential. Most kids in this country before the First World War didn't finish elementary school before going to work. To be fair, my grandmother also had mad typing skills. Even on those old, mechanical typewriters she could hit 60 words per minute. She made a living as a secretary for over 70 years.

A generation later, a woman needed a high school diploma if she was going to find work in an office. A high school diploma set her apart, made her "better than the average bear."

A generation ago, the ante was raised again. Now an undergraduate degree was the cost of entry. A high school diploma no longer conferred an advantage, set you apart. A college degree could set you up for enough interviews to land a job.

Today, kids with college degrees are as ubiquitous as kudzu, if more attractive. An undergraduate degree allows the typical 22-year-old to ask, "Do you want fries with that?"

It's true that a college grad makes more money over the course of a lifetime than a high school grad. It is also true that no one can live on the earnings of a college grad. Not in 2017. For any kind of employment that can lead to a debt-free life, a graduate degree is a must.

Sure, there are some four-year degrees that lead directly to jobs. As of this writing, engineering of all kinds, accounting, and actuarial science all confer employable skills. Of the 20 highest paying jobs for

college grads, 14 of them were in some kind of engineering. Bad news for those of us who aren't "math-y". Good news for everybody who acknowledges that graduate school is the way to go.

The take away is that only the last degree matters. An over-priced undergraduate degree may be an absurd expenditure. Being graduated with untenable debt even more ill advised. Where you go—especially HSCs—may be an expensive mistake. Going to the right school, not the name school, makes the most sense economically and emotionally.

Chapter 21

HOW DO I GET TO CARNEGIE HALL?

I T'S THE LAST DEGREE THAT MATTERS. Where you went to undergraduate school makes no difference. Yale Law School admits kids from colleges that you have never heard of. What more proof do you need that where you go is not nearly as important as who you are?

What do I mean by "schools you've never heard of"? Let's consider the list of where Yale Law School kids did their undergraduate studies. Yes, Yale Law School accepted students last year who did their first four years at big name schools—Amherst and Bowdoin, Duke and Georgetown. But not everyone scurrying off to New Haven for three years of reading cases went to selective schools. Yale Law also shined an acceptance on students from the University of Alabama, the University of Arkansas, and Mississippi State University. Maybe you've heard of the University of Alabama. My wife's cousin teaches there and I'm told that they have a well-known football program. But what about Georgia State University? Ever heard of it? Not the University of Georgia in Athens where the Bulldogs play, but GSU in Atlanta which accepts 58% of its applicants.

Georgia State is not well known but they are sending a student to Yale Law School.

Wanna play again? The year before last, Yale Law School admitted a student who was an undergraduate at Patrick Henry University. You've never heard of Patrick Henry University? Maybe I shouldn't admit this, but I have been doing undergraduate admissions counseling for over three decades and I'VE NEVER HEARD OF PATRICK HENRY UNIVERSITY EITHER. Patrick Henry University, in Purcellville, Virginia admitted 95% of its applicants last year. Of the fifty-something graduates—it's a small school—one of them was accepted at Yale Law. That's right. About two percent (one out of 50) of the graduating class of Patrick Henry University is going to New Haven to study law. Two percent of the graduating class at Harvard (two percent of 2000 is 40) is doing no such thing.

Please do not misconstrue the above. I am not suggesting that the  way to get into a highly competitive graduate school is to attend a highly non-competitive undergraduate school. But the data is unequivocal: with a 90th percentile LSAT score and a B- average from Harvard undergrad, your child is unlikely to be admitted to an accredited law school in the United States. With a 90th percentile LSAT score and an A+ average from Loyola of Chicago, your child may have a shot at attending Yale Law School. As indeed, someone did. That's right: Loyola of Chicago, a school that admits 71% of its applicants, is sending a graduate to Yale Law.

What else do we know about the student who was undergrad at Patrick Henry University before going on to Yale for law school? Absolutely nothing. Like I said, I had never even heard of Patrick Henry University before researching it for this chapter. But I'm going to make a couple inferences. First, I'm going to give her a name, Pat. Now I'm going to make some guesses. I suspect that Pat got pretty much all As in her classes in her first four years of college at Patrick Henry University. I also expect that Pat didn't decide where to attend undergraduate school based on name recognition.

As far as name recognition goes, now that Pat is at Yale Law School, she will have the opportunity to make up for lost time in the name recognition category.

For the rest of her life.

Chapter 22

TRAGEDY

T HE FOLLOWING NOTES ARE TAKEN from a senior in high school whom I counseled recently. It took us some time to help her get her sense of herself back. Realizing that she didn't have to apply only to HSCs was a big first step.

"I just got my SATs back: 680 math which is terrible; 650 critical reading which is even worse. I just don't see myself getting into any of the schools I'm interested in. My counselor at school says that I don't have a chance at Brown, that there is no point in even applying. My counselor at school said the same thing about all the colleges I like. What's the point of even spending the money on the application fees if I won't get in? I'm taking four AP classes, studying between four and five hours every night–more on the weekends—doing the best I can but I just don't see anything good coming out of it long term. Yes, I have all As, but I got a B in AP History last year; all the other kids have better grades and harder classes. I'm the leading scorer on the soccer team, but we lost in the finals of the state tournament last year. I guess I'm lucky that my grandparents put away money for college and I can afford to go anywhere, but I'm not sure what good the money will do because I just know I won't get in. As soon as I saw my scores, I knew I had failed and failed miserably."

"Indeed, everything about me is completely and utterly wrong."

Every decent person who loves kids will take issue with each and every implication in the above paragraph. Let us with one voice affirm the following:

1) Her scores are fine. There are any number of wonderful colleges that would be happy to have a student with this profile: 1300 SATs; 3.8 unweighted GPA; soccer star; and full pay to boot.

2) Everyone—young women in particular—wishes she had done better on the SAT.

3) Studying four or five hours a day is plenty.

4) Applications cost about fifty bucks (The University of Florida is only $30; Tufts, outside Boston, is $70.) You wouldn't gamble fifty thousand dollars if you perceive that your odds are bad, but fifty bucks isn't enough to get the family out of Chicken Kitchen at dinnertime. There's no reason not to take a shot at one or two "reach" schools.

5) In *Reviving Ophelia: Saving the Selves of Adolescent Girls*, Mary Pipher points out that the White Rock mineral water girl in 1954 was 5'4" and weighed 140 pounds. Forty years later, the girl in the advert was 5' 10" and 110 pounds. Simple arithmetic extrapolation to 2017, gives us a 6' 1" tall girl who weighs 95 pounds, basically a stick with boobs. No one looks like this. No one healthy anyway. At this rate, by 2044, the girl would be 6' 7' and weigh 65 pounds, so my argument may not be perfect. But you get the point.

6) "In all the years I've been a therapist," Pipher goes on to say, "I've yet to meet one girl who likes her body... They have been culturally conditioned to hate their bodies, which are, after all, themselves." Isn't the metaphor for SATs, which the girls accept as a proxy for their minds, just as cogent? The girls look in the cognitive mirror and, no matter what they see, they are disappointed and dissatisfied. In all the years I've been counseling, I've never met a girl who liked her scores.

7) The science of understanding and treating girls who self-harm is still in its infancy. Even the best mental health professionals aren't in clear agreement on where eating disorders or cutting behaviors come from or how to help the girls who suffer with these life-threatening

maladies. But wouldn't you guess that a girl who hates herself is more likely to cut herself? Wouldn't you guess that a girl who likes her body and likes her scores would be less likely to be promiscuous, throw up after meals, ingest random drugs, run away from home, and engage in other risky behaviors? My gentle advice for loving parents is simple: love your kids for who they are. Not for what they look like. Not for what they got on their SATs. Because, really, how are you going to find clothes for a 6' 7" daughter who weighs 65 pounds?

Most importantly, lessen the stress in your home. Encourage your daughters to apply to some non-HSCs. They will be happier in the short term and better served for the rest of their lives.

Chapter 23

PSYCHIC DAMAGE TO CHILD: YOU'RE NOT OK AS YOU ARE

"**H**OW HAS THE COLLEGE ADMISSIONS process changed in the 30-something years that I have been helping students choose and apply to college?"
When I meet with students and families, I typically point out how students are filling in more applications and that therefore it's harder to predict who will be admitted where. I talk about "yield"—the number of admitted students who actually matriculate. If Tommy applies to 12 colleges and is offered a spot at seven of them, there are six schools where he doesn't show up. It's increasingly hard for those seven schools to make good predictions about the size of their first year classes.

The Common Application has its pluses, but allowing colleges to know who is likely to be on-campus the following fall is not one of them. A generation ago, filling in an application by hand or with a typewriter was a commitment. Remember trying to line up your answers to "name," "address," and "phone number" on your portable selectric? Remember white out? Remember tearing up the mangled application and getting up the courage to write to the college to request another copy?

But the biggest change since I started advising families in 1983 is that parents no longer even pretend to be subtle about their perception of college admissions as an arms race. "Duke or Die!" is ingrained in both generations. Perhaps, as a result of the stress, parents don't even pretend to model ethical behavior in the admissions process.

Frankie, a good student, mentions that he was the treasurer of the Future Business Leaders of America Club at his private school.

"Write down that you were president," his unblinking mother says.

"But I wasn't president, mom," Frankie replies. His mom continues: "How would they know?"

Of course, I found the above conversation horrifying. Poor Frankie, who now has to contradict his mother in order to fill in an accurate application. And poor Frankie's mom. What a burden it must be to believe that unless your child is admitted to Duke that his life will be lessened in some way. Imagine teaching your child that it's okay to lie.

I gently explained that independent counselors cannot be part of a process that involves falsifying applications. Frankie's mom just looked at me. Maybe she was waiting for me to wink and say, "Just kidding." Maybe she thought I would ask her for more money. I can think of many meetings over the years that I have enjoyed more.

The good news is that there is a big win for families who are willing to go about the process of filling in applications in an appropriate way.

If you refuse to encourage your children to exaggerate, prevaricate, and fib on their applications, there is less likelihood that they will grow up to be criminal psychopaths arrested and imprisoned for stealing pension funds.

Kohlberg taught us about the stages of moral development. A young child might not steal a cookie for fear of getting caught. An older child might not steal a cookie considering that there might not be enough cookies for everyone. I would argue that Frankie's mom clearly wants all the cookies for herself.

Kids learn what they live. Model joy, acceptance. "Don't do things. Be things." Communicate that your kids will be okay if they go to Duke or some "lesser" school. Let your kids know that you believe in them because they have your good values and morals.

Kids who get screamed at learn how to get screamed at or how to scream. Abused kids learn how to be abused or how to abuse. And kids who are taught to lie learn how to lie. On the other hand, kids who are respected learn how to be respectful.

How do loving parents bring up healthy kids in a world overrun with people like Frankie's mom? Communicate to your kids at every opportunity: I love you for who you are, not for what you do. You are my beloved child whether you are admitted to this college or that. And in our family, behaving honorably is more important than being president of the Future Business Leaders of America.

If instead, you communicate to your child that where she goes to school is more important than who she is, cheating will likely be just one of many intractable problems.

Chapter 24

ANOTHER REAL LIFE TRAGIC EXAMPLE

THE EMPHASIS ON ADMISSION TO HSCS can lead to many an absurd stop on the road to nowhere. I wish the parents in the following session were fictional instead of common.

Theresa 's 11th grade transcript was admirable: Advanced Placement courses in chemistry, American History, and English each with a grade of A. Her SATs were strong, her ACTs even stronger. Although she was uncomfortable with her extra-curriculars, endless hours volunteering as a math tutor, I was able to reassure her that even were she a bouzouki player or captain of the underwater rugby team that admission to HSCs is never a slam dunk and that her profile put her "in the pot." That is to say, she had about an 8% chance of being admitted to schools that admit about 8% of their applicants.

Before I could even attempt to assuage her anxiety further, by explaining that "Dartmouth or Die" is a no-win way of walking through the transition process, her dad spoke up. He was concerned—"frenetic" is harder for me to spell—about his daughter's grade point average. Theresa's unweighted 3.7 weighed heavily on his soul. He explained how his daughter had taken two courses at North Cornstalk State, the local community college, but had received Bs in both. "Our strategy exploded horribly," he explained.

Unable to perceive any shrapnel or shattered lives in my office, I tried to massage the conversation around to learning rather than credentialing. Silly me. I inelegantly inquired whether Theresa had enjoyed her advanced courses at the college—her Bs notwithstanding.

All three family members went nacoleptically silent. "What courses did you take?" I blundered on. "You're an advanced math student. Having taken all the courses—BC calculus and AP statistics—that your high school has to offer, did you go on to differential equations at the college?"

After glancing at her parents, Theresa spoke up: "I took introductory Spanish and an algebra I course."

Pushing my befuddled foot still deeper into my gaping mouth, I continued, "But you have native fluency in Spanish and you mastered the algebra I curriculum three years ago."

Again, the family was loudly silent. Had I asked them to do the chicken dance? Did somebody die? Finally Theresa's dad spoke up. "We had heard that admissions to top schools depends on grade point average. So we loaded up on courses where she was sure to get As."

Like Wile E. Coyote who runs off the edge of the cliff but hasn't yet looked down, I still wasn't getting it. Fortunately, dad went on: "But her Spanish teacher found out that Theresa speaks Spanish, so he refused to give her more than a B. And the math teacher did not grade fairly either. Do you think that's just? Why should she be penalized for that which she already knows?"

What isn't fair, I thought to myself, is that this child is being treated like a product rather like an actual human teenager. What isn't fair is that this family is trying to game the system. What isn't fair is that this child views her entire education only as a means to an end.

Can you imagine a native speaker sitting through endless repetitions of "¿Hola, Paco, cómo estás?"

Just to pad a transcript which, from the look of it, didn't need any padding? But if the purpose of sending this kid to the community college to sit through courses from which she could not possibly learn anything was to communicate to Theresa 1) that she wasn't okay as she was and 2) that admissions is a game to be played not a match to be made, then perhaps she got that message loud and clear.

Look, I'm not a zealot. I don't spend weekday mornings in the park slobbering about how a child will learn more from reading an actual book than from doing yet another vapid worksheet. I don't drone on about how the agenda in many high schools is about power and control rather than learning that which might be intrinsically motivating, beautiful, or even—perish forbid!—useful. Although I have been known to give a student or two a book or two over the years, I am not one of those "outside agitators" referenced in "The Graduate."

But—speaking of movies—I do remember Ben Stein's great homage to horrific teachers everywhere in "Ferris Beuler's Day Off" in which no one responds to his questions.

"... The great depression. (Pause.) Passed the... Anyone? (Pause.) The Hawley-Smoot Tariff Act. Which raised or lowered? (Pause.) Raised tariffs in an effort to collect... (Pause.) More government revenue..."

Surely, we can do better than that.

Last point: Clearly, earning $60,000 a year is "better" in every meaningful definition of the word than earning $40,000, don't you agree? You can buy more food with the extra twenty thousand dollars and not worry so much about finances. But is earning $60,000,000 a year so much more important than earning $40,000,000? Don't you think you could somehow manage to stumble through with a lousy $40M? How much is enough? What is the cost of that extra money? What is the value of that extra .1 of gpa?

A 3.8 rather than a 3.7 unweighted gpa doesn't significantly affect Theresa's admissibility at "top" schools or harm her in any way. But viewing her education as something that is done to her over which she has no control does not do her any good. There has got to be something wrong about a bilingual kid listening endlessly to "Muy bien. ¿Y usted?"

If her parents could come to understand that who she is makes more difference than where she goes, pointless suffering could have been avoided.

Chapter 25

I WOULD WRITE LESS ABOUT CHEATING IF THERE WERE LESS OF IT

REMEMBER THAT KID WHO INVENTED all those brilliant ways to cheat in high school? Even before electronic communications, he was making crib sheets in ingenious ways. Writing information on his sleeve, hiding notes in his sneakers, there was nothing he wouldn't do.

Except study, of course.

Parents today have stolen a page from the playbook of our young fraud. If headlines are to be believed, these misguided folks are now shelling out tens

or even hundreds of thousands of dollars to hucksters who profess to have the formula for admissions to highly selective colleges.

What is a top college according to the silliness? One that is high in the rankings of that absurd and—on my street—largely discredited magazine. Fallacy tottering on fallacy. By this logic, why not rank women (or men) from most to least desirable? Ignoring individual differences would allow us all to double the money we spend on a college education and pursue the same people. (Needless to say, I believe that my lovely wife would top the charts ahead of Sophia Vergara and Jennifer Aniston, but I'll have to wait for the formula to be quantified and the magazine to be published to be certain of where she stands.)

For every thousand dollars these parents spend gaming the college admissions process, they should instead take their kids camping (or for a walk on the beach or to the library or to the scrap-booking store or to the home of an elderly neighbor to drop off some homemade cookies.) The investment will pay off in every more meaningful way.

Because the research is unequivocal: who you are matters more than where you go. Kids with ability, whether they go to colleges that admit 6% or 60% of their applicants, end up the same; they do fine independent of the name on the sweatshirt. Kids without ability don't do well. Again, it doesn't matter nearly as much where they go to school.

Of course "ability" is a hard deer to hunt, a tricky term to define. But in this context ability might be defined as "knowing that the test is next Monday, but that there is a paper due next Tuesday and that putting off starting the paper until after the exam will leave only one day to write it which isn't enough so I better shut down the text function on my phone and make an appointment to see the professor to run an idea by her and then I better make a few tuna sandwiches because it's going to be a long night in the library because this is a tough course

and I know that I'm going to have to read the chapter twice and it looks like I'm going to miss the pep rally for the football game."

Kids who are able to delay gratification, organize their time, prioritize, seek help, plan ahead, and take responsibility for their process do well. Kids who are able to acknowledge, embrace, and articulate their learning styles do well. Kids who know that they can read 15 pages an hour of a complicated text book and that they can study for three hours before their brain turns to mush and they need a break also do well.

This is not news.

Kids who stop playing "League of Legends" at one in the morning, so they can get the reading done for their nine a. m. class? Kids who smoke pot and forget they have a paper due? Kids who lie to their professors, lie to their parents, and lie to themselves about how much they are studying? Kids who don't know to ask for help to get their stuff done? They do less well.

I met a seemingly well-intentioned father the other day who was ready to write a check for two million dollars to facilitate his child's admission to a "top" school. I could not help but wonder how much he was willing to spend to keep her there.

Here's a not so secret formula: stop spending time, effort, and money on worrying about where your children will go to college. Invest your treasure on focusing on who your children are.

Because no matter where you go, there you are.

Oh, and here's the "secret" of the "success" of the scam artist charging hundreds of thousands of dollars purporting to have cracked the formula for admission to top colleges.

This swindle has been around since the 30s but every generation brings newer and more naive sheep. The independent counselor promises to "get your child in" to a top college or your money back. This time the fraud has a "formula;" years ago he "knew someone" in admissions. Either way, the promise of "I'll get your kid in to a top college or your money back" is made to a number of feckless families. Statistically, some of them get in. Princeton, Harvard, and Stanford all admit fewer than one student in ten but SOMEBODY gets in. The huckster tells your kid to play the tuba or to volunteer at the nursing home. Or he gives your kid some magic beans.

In any case, if the student doesn't get admitted to a "top" school, the parents get their money back. If the kid does get admitted the slime-oid laughs all the way to the safety deposit box. It doesn't take too many $200,000 payouts to make a good, if despicable, living.

In the meantime, hard-working, ethical counselors across the country will continue to spread the message: there is no formula that guarantees admission to "top" colleges.

And who your kid is matters more than where she goes.

Chapter 26

THE ADMISSIONS PROCESS AND THE WEDDING SPEECH

H ERE IS YET ANOTHER REASON TO focus on the needs of the child rather than the location of the college.

Given how busy everyone is lately I thought I might take the liberty of writing a couple of speeches for you. I know it may seem like the wedding of your son is some years away, but tempus seems to keep on fugiting, whatever that means, so let's not wait to the last minute like you did with those college admissions essays, shall we?

Here are two possible toasts. Tell me which one you look forward to reciting at the meal after the ceremony.

1) "Ladies and gentlemen, could I have your attention, please? Thank you so much. You know, speaking of attention, I thought this guy here would never graduate from high school given how severely attention deficit and hyperactive he was. Yeah, we butted heads year in and year out.

I remember the time I told him to do his homework or else get the hell out of the house and we got in a fist fight so he went to live under a bridge for a few weeks. Yeah, I thought HRS would never leave us alone. But things worked out after the law suits settled and I stapled my son's legs to a chair. He finally got the proper academic credentials and is now an associate at Hummadinger and Dreck although we don't speak more than twice a year."

2) Almost anything else. Maybe something involving joy. You  don't want to look back on the years from toddlerhood through early 20s as an unrelenting series of unpleasant conversations in which your dissatisfaction with who your kid is and what he does is the only communication. "Do your homework! Read a book! Write that admissions essay!"

Let me be more specific. Parents spend a tremendous amount of time telling their kids what to do, what to think, what to feel. Some of this information is doubtless useful—put your shoes on, get a vaccination, go to college. But some of it, I might argue, is a bit over the top. I hear stories about parents who do homework for their kids. I hear rumors about parents who write college application essays for their offspring. I'm told that there are parents who spend more time working on their children's resumes than they do talking to their actual children.

Dr. Spock's Baby and Child Care was first published just after the war. By the time of Dr. Spock's death in 1998, 50 million copies had been sold. The book has insight into feeding schedules, potty training, dog bites, and tantrums. But the best advice of all remains, "put down the book, pick up the baby." Similarly, for parents concerned about college applications, gentle guidance might include, "focus on the child, not on the college."

Because a kid who has skills will do well wherever she matriculates. You heard it here first: a child who knows how to study and is relatively free of process addictions will do fine in the classroom and out. Okay, you didn't hear it here first. The research is clear. Kids who have the ability (time management, study skills, motivation) to go to "top" schools but choose State U instead go on to professional school just as frequently as if they ended up with a big name sweatshirt.

And what could you do with all the time NOT spent padding the resume? What could you do with the time NOT committed to graduating at the top of your class? You and your son could hike a significant portion of the Appalachian Trail. (Admission: Free.) You and your son could attend every baseball game of that small college near your home. (Tickets, third base side, eight dollars each.) You and your son could buy copies of *The Amazing Spiderman* issues 50 through 100. (In good condition, these issues typically go for $30 or $40 each. You could buy them all for less than what you were going to spend on preparation for the SAT.) In short, you and your son could spend some no agenda time together, silently enjoying one another's company.

And wouldn't THAT be something to talk about during the toast at your son's wedding?

Chapter 27

JEFFERSON ON EDUCATION

"Educate and inform the whole mass of the people... They are the only sure reliance for the preservation of our liberty." — T. Jefferson

T HAT'S AS MAY BE, BUT THE ISSUE OF who who gets educated where remains unresolved 200 years after Jefferson wrote about our fledgling democracy. It is not news that those from enriched environments are more

likely to get a jump on the prospect of superior venues and results. Kids who grow up with a bath of language have an advantage over those whose baby sitters are glowing rectangles.

One of my colleagues at a competitive day school was my student years ago. She doesn't give me insider information based on our long-standing relationship. Nor does she give preference to students whom I counsel. She does speak to me plainly without the euphemisms and edubabble that characterize much of the communication between admissions offices and the broader culture.

"If a child from an enriched background doesn't score in the 90thpercentile on norm referenced tests, we are hard pressed to offer him a place in the sixth grade class," Nicole has told me over the decades. "We just have too many kids with high scores. We have to make some guesses about who is going to perform."

The disconnect for me is that the headmaster of Nicole's school brags incessantly about the results of their students. "Of the one hundred seniors at Barrister and Thistledown last year, 94 of them took at least one advanced placement course and 52 of them took three of more AP tests. The number of students who earned a passing score (a 3 or above on a scale of 5) numbered over 80%."

The headmaster pauses as if revealing the winning lotto numbers from the drawing next week: "Last year thirty percent of B & T graduates were admitted to Ivy League schools" he says, his voice a throaty whisper.

Perhaps the following simple analogy will make my exasperation apparent: Imagine two hospitals, both of which admitted a thousand patients this month. At Hospital A, 179 of those patients died. At Hospital B, 23 people died.

Which is the better hospital?

For those of you who said Hospital A because 179 is a bigger number than 23, I have two questions, only one of which is snarky and rude:

1) Do you think I have so little respect for my gentle readers to ask a question with such a simple, obvious answer? I have counseled hundreds of students over the past 30 plus years. I have written over 300 blog posts for goodness sake. I am honored to have thousands of good folks graciously consider my musings each week. Did I attract such a large following by wasting the time of the good folks who are kind enough to consider my thoughts?

Certainly not!

What if Hospital A works with victims of violence, gun shot wounds, construction accidents, and car crashes while Hospital B does tummy tucks, Botox injections, and boob jobs? Wouldn't you expect a higher mortality rate at the hospital 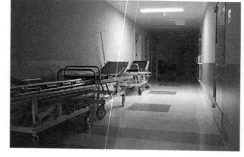 working with the desperately injured, half-dead? If you took those unfortunates with the severed limbs to Hospital B, you can bet more than just 179 of them would die. Without trauma surgeons, reserves of blood products, and the Jaws of Life, those poor folks wouldn't have a snow-ball's chance. Hospital A is the better hospital. Unless you have terminal wrinkles on your fore-head.

Similarly, bragging about college placement statistics is misleading. Given the best of the best among sixth grade applicants, it is no surprise that those kiddos end up with good scores and admissions to top schools six years later.

Of course those kids do well. Why wouldn't they?

"Of the boys thus sent in any one year, trial is to be made at the grammar schools one or two years, and the best genius of the whole selected, and continued six years, and the residue dismissed. By this means twenty of the best geniusses (sic) will be raked from the rubbish annually..."

Thomas Jefferson, the father of democracy, considered picking the number of kids who fit in one classroom today from a population of hundreds of kids. The rest were to be "dismissed." The question today revolves around what to do with those who have been dismissed. Pretending that the "top" schools produce top kids is as absurd as suggesting that Hospital A kills patients. What to do with the vast majority of kids who aren't in the top ten percent remains a question.

If it turns out that your kid is not one of the selected few attending Barrister and Thistledown, then accepting and loving her for who she is rather than beating her up for not being someone else would be a great first step.

Acknowledging that who she is matters more than where she goes would make sense also.

Chapter 28

TUITION

HOW DO PRIVATE SCHOOLS JUSTIFY tuition? Magnet public schools the same thing. You don't think neighborhood schools are playing the same game? There's not much honesty left in the process. Few high school college counselors are having transparent conversations with colleagues on the college side. Few high school counselors are saying "don't write this down" and telling the truth about a kid who is a grade grubber or is on the autism spectrum.

Similarly, college admissions folks aren't telling the truth either. Not like in generations past. Admissions used to be about counseling. Now it's about enrollment management. Careers are made based on the number of applications. Promotions are determined by "yield"— the number of admitted kids who show up. "Your interests would be better served elsewhere, Son" are words no college admissions person ever spoke. Not in the last 30 or 40 years anyway.

Why are the number of kids who apply and the number of admitted kids who show up so important? In detective novels from the 50s, "cherchez le femme." In admissions today, follow the dollars. Colleges are able to borrow money with which to build buildings based on a rating from a bond agency. The rating determines interest rate. The rating is based on—you guessed it—the number of applicants and the percentage of yield. A college admissions counselor who tells a kid the truth is cutting her own throat. She can't say, "you won't be happy here." She has to say, "Yes, please apply. We'll give your application every consideration." Even if she knows the kid has zero chance of being admitted and a less than zero chance of being successful if she were. The more applicants the better. That's where the rating come from. It's an arms race.

Some years ago The University of Chicago admitted 80% of its applicants. (see Chapter 12.) Pretty much everybody who filled in an application was accepted. Everybody knew the deal. UC was intensely academic. Half the faculty had a Nobel prize. (Okay, I made that up but you get the point.) Classes were intellectually rigorous. Brilliant kids studied hard and learned a ton. Many students went on to academic careers of their own. There was a clear selection bias in the application process. Only intellectually curious kids who could do the work applied to Chicago.

Not any more. Because Chicago is subject to the same economic pressures as every other institution; they need more applicants. They need to be able to reject a bunch of kids. So Chicago sent out some postcards with pretty pictures of clean classrooms and smiling undergraduates. "Please apply!" And lots of kids did. Kids who would have been miserable at Chicago saw the postcard with the clean classrooms and the smiling undergrads and filled in aps. "Chicago sent me a postcard," the kids exclaimed. They must want me!

Not so much.

Of course those kids weren't admitted. Chicago continued to accept the same students that it had for decades, the same brilliant hard working kids. The only difference was that, thanks to the postcards, the University of Chicago now rejects scads of applicants. Their admit ratio went from 80% (pretty much everybody got in) to a respectable 8% (Good luck, Charlie Brown.)

The admit ratio went down; Chicago gets a higher rating for bonds; everybody wins.

Except of course the students.

How can your child avoid the madness? How can you help you child not be scammed by marketing departments that have no relationship to what goes on at the college itself? How can you help your kids focus on their education rather than on misguided ranking designed only to sell magazines? By realizing that having the skill to be a Chicago kid is more important than actually being a University of Chicago kid. Who they are is more important than where they go.

Chapter 29

CHEATING PART SIX.
HIGH SCHOOL COUNSELORS
JOIN IN

> Here's a biology joke:
> "A chicken is an egg's way
> of making another egg."

HERE'S A SIGNIFICANTLY LESS AMUSING aspect of how the madness surrounding admissions to highly selective colleges has trickled down to the high school. "How does a high school attract another student?" Let's consider the tuition numbers before determining the answer. An independent day school in a metropolitan area charges upwards of $30K/year. Tra-

ditional boarding schools have tuitions north of $50K/year. Boarding schools for students with learning differences get $70,000/year. Boarding schools for students with learning differences and behavioral issues bill $120,000/year. How are these tuitions justified?

Schools can argue that the class selections are varied, the teachers learned and compassionate, the facilities modern and clean. Schools can point to the number of books in the library or the number of 3-D printers in the lab. Schools can show off the robotics lab and the number of practice pianos. Schools can (and do) mention the percentage of faculty who have advanced degrees. Schools can (and should) point out how small the class sizes are and how the teachers are available for extra help. If your kid fits in and can function then the choice of high school makes no difference in the college admissions process. Day schools are great; boarding schools are great; public schools are great. The first year seminar at HSCs are filled with kids from every type of high school. So how do parents justify choosing the private school or the boarding school over the public school? How do families determine that the money is well spent? At some point every parent of a prospective fee-paying student asks, "where do your graduates go to college?" If the answer is "The University of Denver, Northern Michigan, and Oregon..." (see chapter 8) then the parents are going to keep shopping. "Where our students are going to college" is what sells. The way independent schools and boarding schools attract next year's crop of students is by showing off the list of top name colleges to which their current students are heading. "Oh, so your students typically matriculate at Harvard, Stanford, and Duke?" intone prospective parents. "Then our child simply must attend high school here. May I write you a check?"

Which puts the counselors employed by the high schools in a sticky position.

Years ago, the allegiance of the high school counselor was with the colleges specifically and education in general. Counselors told the truth as they saw it: "Susie would be a good fit for Yale; Tommy not so much." Admissions counselors, before they became part of the "enrollment management team," told the truth as well. "Susie, we're glad you applied. Tommy, I think your needs would be better met elsewhere." Teachers, administrators, counselors, and even families were on the same page. "Admissions is a match to be made, not a prize to be won."

No longer.

It is now the counselor's job to advocate for each and every student at his expensive, tuition driven high school. A chicken is an egg's way of making another egg. A list of highly competitive schools to which our kids have been admitted is a high school's way of attractive another student. If the counselor tells the truth on the recommendation, "Tommy is a nice kid but he has neither the ability nor the motivation to do well at your school," the counselor can count on two guaranteed outcomes: the counselor's honesty will be appreciated by the highly selective college trying to determine which of the ten kids to admit for the one opening; the counselor will be looking for a job come February.

So high school counselors prevaricate. They use euphemisms. They suggest that "William is focused on his studies" rather than "William is a grade grubbing little snot who refuses to be part of study group because he is only interested in his own success." High school counselors can certainly no longer call a colleague on the college side and say, "Hi, Jim. Don't write this down, but I feel pretty strongly that Tommy cheated on every test on which he ever got a passing grade."

Counselors have every reason to cheat. Which is not to say that all of them do. High school counselors put themselves at risk for unemployment if they tell the truth about students. The pressure from the administration is clear: our graduates need to be admitted to highly selective schools; otherwise we may ALL be looking for jobs. There

is a line between "I've never seen you looking so lovely" and "Boy, does that dress make you look unattractive." Here is an example of unethical advice that clearly crosses the line, advice that is so egregious that it shames honorable counselors everywhere.

"Say I've got a kid who wants to get into Clemson—and it's ridiculously hard to get into Clemson—I tell him: You're going to major in turf-grass management. They're always looking for kids in that major. And then, once you're in, if you want you can be like 80 percent of college students and CHANGE. YOUR. MAJOR." (Emphasis in the original.)

In case the message of the quote above isn't clear on its face, I will summarize: "Lie. Lie on your application to college."

If teaching your kids how to lie to achieve their dubious aims is your goal, you might be reading the wrong book. Let's assume to the contrary that you want your kids to grow up not to be liars. How might sensible parents avoid inspiring their kids to lie?

1) Teach your kids to tell the truth. Encourage them to tell the truth on their applications to college. Allow your kids to tell the truth in all aspects of their lives. Inspire them to tell the truth in all circumstances except when to lie would be hurtful. "You look GREAT in that sari;

you should certainly wear it on your date," for example.

2) Get off the train. Don't play the game. Don't worry about whether or not your kid will be admitted to Clemson. If your kid has SKILLS and goes somewhere other than Clemson, she will end up just where she needs to be.

If you must teach your children to lie, at least come up with a lie that has some likelihood however small of being successful. Clemson University was founded in 1889. Do you think there's any possibility that their admissions office doesn't know about the turf management lie? "Hmm, we got a tough call here," says the director of admissions at Clemson. "This kid has never taken a science course that wasn't required and has no extra-curriculars that suggest the least interest in agriculture. OMG, wait a minute! He says he wants to major in turf management! Let's admit him!" Not a chance.

The broader point, as always, is that there is something to be said for raising a child whose first thought is not "I know, I'll tell a lie." Looking beyond obsessing about highly competitive colleges is the place to start. By all means apply to the HCSs of your choice. Just tell the truth on your applications and understand that you may or may not be admitted.

Chapter 30

SATIRIC ESSAY ON WHY CHEATING IS A DESPERATELY ILL —ADVISED STRATEGY

I DON'T WANT TO GIVE TOO MANY DETAILS. I'm not saying this is a good idea what I did, only that it can happen. I know it can happen and how it happened because I did it. I'm not saying that I would want anyone to follow this exact path or that it was a good idea and I guess maybe I cut some corners. I suppose you could say that what I did was wrong.

It started when I was a high school athlete. Again without being too specific, let's just say my dad knew the coach. I'm not saying influence was involved; I'm not saying it wasn't. Anyway, I got to be on the football team instead of some other guys who maybe had a little more ability or worked a little harder.

I guess college was a similar circumstance. I made the team at a Division One school. Sure there were other guys who were faster, stronger, more experienced, and better players all around. But sometimes you have to do what you have to do, right?

The end justifies the means or something like that. So I sent the coach some videotape that have me running 40 yards in 4.2 seconds. And I got a doctor to sign off on my being able to bench press 225 pounds 47 times. Maybe the doctor owed my dad a favor. Maybe the tape wasn't exactly accurate. Four point two seconds may have been something of an exaggeration. It is no exaggeration to say that I took every human growth hormone, steroid, injection and illegal performance enhancing drug I could find. I hired a doctor to give me some other drugs so that the illegal drugs I took couldn't be detected.

Again, I don't want to give away too many of the details. Let's  just say that I was drafted to play in the NFL and made the team. Through some fairly sophisticated subterfuge, I got through training camp. I used a stunt double and I talked my way through some stuff with the coaches who relied on my fake videos and some other tricky stuff.

So now the first game is in a few minutes and I'm thinking about how I've never actually played any football. I'll be lining up opposite Randy Stark. He's the 6'3", 305 pound starting defensive tackle for the Miami Dolphins. He actually can do 37 bench press repeats at 225 pounds. Actually, he's kind of a beast. The truth of the matter is that I am 5' 10" and weigh 175 pounds.

How do you think I'm going to do against Randy Stark in the game?

Laura's parents really, truly, and desperately want her to attend the California Institute of Technology. That's where they both went, where they met. Laura's parents are willing to do anything for her to go there. Her parents believe strongly that Laura's best chance of meeting a man who will be successful is by attending Cal Tech.

Laura's grades are above average, although she is struggling in her senior year of math, pre-calculus. She has friends, some of whom are also applying to Cal Tech—who are two years ahead of her in math and are sailing through advanced placement calculus BC. A few of her friends, also still in high school, are taking differential equations at the University. Laura has a 580 on the SAT. The math SAT score for matriculating students at Cal Tech is some 200 points higher. Laura reluctantly studies an hour and a half each day. Most students at Cal Tech study over three and half hours each day. Laura is reluctant to meet with the tutors whom her parents have hired.

Still, let's say that Laura is admitted. Her parents contribute ten million dollars or fake her transcript or there's a computer glitch or some crazy thing and she gets the "Congratulations" email rather than the "We had too many qualified applicants" one. (I have to ask for a little willing suspension of disbelief here, just like in the implausible football story above.)

Were Laura—with her modest math ability, study skills, attitude, and aptitude—to be admitted to Cal Tech, how well do you think she might be expected to do in a classroom filled with smarter, harder working students? I would suggest that the metaphor of the 175-pound man described above who somehow scammed his way into a professional football uniform is an accurate representation in every particular of how Laura is going to do if she goes to Pasadena.

Metaphorically, Laura is going to have every bone in her body shattered.

The point of going to college isn't just to get in; the point of going to college is stay in. And learn something while you're there. And to study hard and thrive not just survive. And to go to the art museum on-campus and sit down with a professor so you can share a meal, a book, and an idea.

"College admissions is about a match to be made not a prize to be won" remains true throughout my 30-something years in the field.

The take-away for parents is simple and straightforward: Know who your kids are. And love them anyway. If your kid belongs at Cal Tech, encourage her to apply and celebrate her choice if she is admitted. If your kids don't belong at Cal Tech—and with room for just under a thousand undergraduates, most kids don't—be happy for them where ever they end up.

Helping your kids to scam their resumes, inflate their accomplishments, and be admitted to schools where they don't belong is as ill-advised as helping a 5" 10", 175-pound man line up in an NFL game against Randy Starks: a true recipe for sadness.

On the field and in the classroom, there is nothing worse than a bad match.

Chapter 31

SATIRIC ESSAY ON HOW ABSURD PADDING THE RESUME HAS BECOME

REMEMBER READING ABOUT THOSE brutally mistreated Chinese girls of not so many generations ago whose feet were bound with strong straps? For reasons that may not even have been clear at the time, fathers felt that petite feet were attractive or indicative of a social class where the girls didn't have to walk much. Maybe the fathers were happy that their injured daughters couldn't run away and go to medical school. The crippled girls, in needless, constant pain, were less happy.

Apparently, women with three-inch feet were considered attractive. If you read the Wikipedia Article, you'll know as much about bound feet as I do.

Before affecting horror and outrage at another culture and another century, reflect on a frequent series of inquiries that my college counseling colleagues and I encounter from families who want their daughters to attend "top" colleges. After 34 years of counseling, college admissions is a subject that I do profess to know something about.

Dad: We don't want to game the system.

123

(Translation: We want to game the system.)

Ethical College Counselors Everywhere: Um hmm.

Dad: We don't want you to confer an unfair advantage. (Translation: Could you make a few calls?)

Ethical College Counselors Everywhere: Um hmm.

Dad: We just want to know how much of her time should be allocated to playing soccer, running for student counsel, editing the student newspaper, building robots, playing the bouzouki, hang gliding, Cotillion lessons, and volunteering at the Whoop Kitchen.

Ethical College Counselors Everywhere: Surely, you mean the "soup" kitchen?

Dad: No, all the positions at the soup kitchen were taken so our daughter cheers and hollers for the girls who do the actual serving. "Way to go! Serve that soup!" That sort of thing. She gets the same number of community service hours though so it doesn't matter.

ECCE: Doesn't matter to whom?

Dad: Sometimes she tries to fall asleep when she studies after all these activities but my wife and I poke her with a stick to keep her awake and focused.

ECCE: You poke your daughter with a stick so she can stay awake and study after being involved in all those time-consuming activities after school?

Dad: Yes, we tried hooking her up to an IV glucose solution when her energy ran low, but her arm got infected from the needle sticks.

ECCE: Her arm got infected?

Dad: She plays soccer. Weren't you listening? Her arms don't matter; the girls kick the soccer ball with their feet. We want to give her the best chance of being admitted to a top college where she will likely meet a man who can provide for her in the fashion to which we insist that she continue to be accustomed.

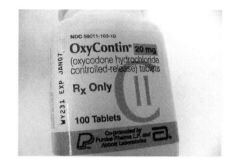

ECCE: Which of those activities is she passionate about?

Dad: None of them, if you must know. She likes art. Why do you ask?

After listening to this dad, is the analogy with the tortuously bound feet seeming a little less outrageous?

And what guesses would you make about this young woman's relationship with her father down the road—whether or not she achieves his dream of being admitted to a top college and marrying a wealthy man?

But shouldn't children work hard, strive for the best, listen to their parents, and do what they're told?

I don't know. I do know that if I had to choose, I'd rather have a contented child than a successful one. Fortunately, I don't have to choose. Kids who are allowed to follow their own path and "be who they are" are more likely to succeed by every meaningful definition of the word.

I met a high-achieving young woman just the other day as it happens. Four AP classes as a tenth grader, star on her traveling soccer team, high test scores. Interestingly enough, I met her in a rehab facility I was touring in Northern Utah. The young woman had become addicted to meth amphetamine.

I know. I know. Using one example and even hinting that there is a causal connection between the high pressure and the drug use is a cheap shot. Yes, there are pressured kids who succeed just as there are low-achieving kids who also turn to drugs. Using just the one child to

125

make a point is a lousy technique of crumby political campaigns, not a strategy I should use in a thoughtful book like this one.

But that young woman and her accomplishments in the classroom and her struggles on the street really hit home for me.

Before you tell me that there are evils and stressors in the world to which our children must be exposed and that our kids need to be able to deal successfully with stress, let me remind you that there are carcinogens in the world but the existence of these toxins is a poor argument for sending your children to the site of a nuclear disaster.

Chapter 32

YOU'RE A PARENT,
NOT A WICKED WITCH

ORCING YOUR CHILDREN TO STUDY *what* you think they should is as bad as forcing your children to study *where* you think they should—as the following essay will suggest:

Look, nobody is saying that Dorothy had it easy. She had to go a long way round to get back to where she belonged, right? Munchkins, poppies, green horses, were just the beginning. Then that annoying scarecrow telling her to go "both ways"? And don't even get me started about those flying monkeys.

What even my most erudite readers may not know is that a previously unknown manuscript of Frank Baum's hundred year-old story has recently been unearthed—in my very backyard of all places. Can you believe it? I am sure you understand that I am not at liberty to disclose all the details of this archaeological breakthrough which would involve my using phrases including "CIA," "masons," fortuitous coincidences," "manuscript sniffing German shepherds," and "none of this ever actually happened." Though Baum's last draft is incomplete, here are a few of the paragraphs that have been deciphered:

Scene: Castle interior. Stone walls festooned with torches, mold, and pennants of highly competitive colleges.

Wicked Witch: Take organic chemistry next year, my pretty.

Dorothy: Have you read Pride and Prejudice? Don't you just adore Jane Austen? I want to read and study everything she's written.

Wicked Witch: What would you do with an English major, teach?

(Derisive cackle.)

Dorothy: I have always found peace working with charcoal and pastels. I wonder if I could find my true passion with acrylics or oils.

Wicked Witch: Go to medical school! (Hurls flaming fireball.)

Dorothy: I barely got a B in pre-calculus and I studied three hours every day. Math comes hard for me.

Wicked Witch: All the careers and big starting salaries are in computer science! Studying art history is a waste of time and money!

Dorothy: There's no place like Rome. There's no place like Rome.

As I mentioned, not all the pages of this classic have been discovered. The search for the complete manuscript continues. Where will the complete text be found? Is it possible that indeed more of this very conversation is going on in the present day in your home?

Are you encouraging your child—"forcing" is such an ugly word—to study that which she neither enjoys nor for which she has any discernible aptitude?

My gentle sarcasm is not a narrow argument in favor of students choosing the liberal arts over science, technology, engineering, and mathematics. To the contrary, I am virulently in favor of all academic disciplines from anthropology to zoology. My point is simply that for many students choosing to study biochemistry rather than history is a false dichotomy. Students who excel in both disciplines can make

128

an informed choice. More common are students who can do well in some majors or fail in others.

My long-standing and favorite dictum, "love the children you get and you'll get the children you love" can be shortened: let them be who they are. And at the risk of extending this metaphor, you want to be the parent who is attuned to your child's needs. You do not want to be the tornado that rips your child away from where she needs to be, from the place to which she will invariably and rightfully return.

You don't need to discover a manuscript in your backyard to have contented children and peace in your home. Flying monkeys are more likely to enforce compliance than to solidify a loving relationship.

Chapter 33

THIS ROLLER COASTER IS MAKING ME NAUSEOUS

T HERE ARE TWO WAYS TO STOP THE madness. One way is not to get on the train in the first place. The other is to stop focusing on admissions and instead to help your kids develop the abilities that will allow them to be successful. Where ever they go to college.

Like all addictions the best way to stop is not to start. Nobody ever woke up in the morning and said, "I have an idea: I'll start smoking pot after breakfast and with any luck at all, I'll be addicted to Oxycontin by dinner time." It may be something of an exaggeration to suggest that obsessing about being admitted to HSCs involves similar compulsions and bad decisions, but before completely dismissing the idea, consider the definition of addiction. Your average person on the street thinks that addiction to drugs or alcohol is defined by consumption or frequency. My Aunt Mary drinks every day; she must be an

alcoholic. Specialists in the field of addiction medicine know better. An addict who doesn't use for a year and then goes on a three-day bender in which she ignores her family, blacks out, and forgets where she has been and what she has done is more at risk than someone who drinks a bottle of wine every Friday. (Not that I am recommending either, mind you.) What an alcoholic does to get alcohol, what an addict does while under the influence of alcohol, and blackouts are the defining characteristics of alcoholism.

Now consider the family obsessed with admissions to HSCs. An international family paid two million dollars to a fraud who claimed he could get the children admitted to Harvard. What's wrong with that picture? One hardly knows where to begin.

The roller coaster of admissions madness isn't just making you sick; it's killing you. Just as an alcoholic has a life circumscribed by alcohol, kids are obsessing about admissions to the point of ignoring anything else in their lives. Here's the worst of it. High school students constantly evaluate their chances of being admitted to HSCs. Of course the reality is that they have no reasonable way of evaluating their odds. Remember my example of the 20 student folders only one of which will be accepted? If the director of admissions doesn't have a clue as to which kid gets in, how in the world can a kid make any valid inference? Yet kids talk about their likelihood of being admitted ALL THE TIME. Here is a typical well-intentioned high school senior blathering interminable nonsense about her chances of being admitted to an HSC:

"The 25th to 75th percentile range is 720-770 on the EBRW (could we just say "verbal" for goodness sake?) and 720-780 on the math. My 760 on the verbal is toward the top of the range but my 690 on the math is below the 25th percentile. So that's bad. I have five AP classes this year, one more than the average for this college, but one of my AP classes is in environmental science rather than a tougher course like AP physics. Everybody in admissions knows that enviro isn't as rigorous a course. Plus I got a B in AP calculus last year and I'm taking statistics rather than BC calculus this year and that's bad also. Still, I have 400 hours of community service so that should set me apart in a positive way and I am editor of the literary magazine so my chances might not be so so bad. But on the other hand, 23 kids from my high school applied to this college last year and only two were admitted which is around nine percent and the national average is 17% so maybe there is something going on with my high school's relationship with this college…"

And on and on. Endless meaningless analysis. A tale "told by an idiot signifying nothing" would convey more information.

Or as Alex Guinness says at the end of "Bridge Over the River Quai," "Madness."

This poor child is measuring with a micrometer what will be cut with an ax. Trying to make these fine distinctions is loopy when the—forgive me for repeating—DIRECTOR OF ADMISSIONS can't make a rational differentiation between kids with similar profiles. Some kids with these lovely credentials get admitted. Some don't. Obsessing about which way the dice are going to come up doesn't do anything to affect the dice and it destroys the kids.

Even worse: Note that the kid with the lovely profile described above doesn't even know what the 25th to 75th percentile range represents. Are those the scores of kids who applied to the HSC, the scores of kids who were admitted to the HSC, or the scores of the kids who matriculated at the HSC?

This child will get in. Or she won't. Either way, she will be fine. If she gets an unlucky roll of the dice, she'll go somewhere else. Did you look at those credentials? She has taken AP everything. She's obviously motivated and brilliant. What could go wrong?

Other than a psychiatric illness caused by overwhelming stress. This child is at risk of an eating disorder, self-harm, substance abuse and every other bad thing. I am stressed out just writing about her profile. She desperately needs to relax. She's going to be fine.

What's the solution? Easy. Well, easy to proscribe, harder to implement. This high-achieving lovely, hard-working senior needs to forget about her chances of admission and focus instead on enjoying her last year of high school. Rather than calculating and recalculating the odds, she needs to go for a hike with family members and sit looking at the river running down the mountains.

Because what if some charlatan were to pretend that the actual odds of admission were known? Suppose some huckster could look

> **Focusing on learning makes for a content senior year; focusing on the chances of being admitted to a highly selective college leads to indigestion, unhappiness, and missed opportunities.**

into a cracked crystal ball and say, "Woo ooh. The spirits tell me that because you have five AP classes, are editor of the literary magazine, and wear a size seven sneaker, your chances of being admitted to your first choice college are 23%"? What if the crook said the student's odds were five percent? Or 42%? There's no prediction that should change the child's behavior! The child needs to go ahead and apply!

Perhaps the following—admittedly horrible—joke will make the point: Two men stand before a firing squad. Their hands are tied behind their backs. Six men are pointing rifles at their hearts. The lieutenant in charge of the firing squad instructs his men, "Wait!" and goes over to the two men secured to the posts in the ground.

"Before I give the order to shoot," the lieutenant says addressing one of the men, "do you want a blind fold, you cowardly pig?" The lieutenant then punches the man in the mouth.

The first man spits blood at the lieutenant and says, "the hell with your blind fold." He spits at the lieutenant again and says, "and the hell with your mother."

The second man turns to the first and says, "Shh. Don't make trouble."

Given how obscure this joke is, I'm going to explain why it's funny: the men are going to die anyway. They are a minute away from being shot. With six rifles. It doesn't matter whether or not the make any trouble. They can insult the lieutenant's mother. Or not. Their situation cannot possibly be any worse.

Similarly, the young woman has nothing to lose by applying. It doesn't matter what her odds are. If an application fee were ten thousand dollars, she would have to think long and hard about risking that much money on a long shot. But an application fee is affordable. Most colleges charge $50. Tufts is a little higher than the average at $70; the University of Florida a little lower at $30. The applicant's family can't have dinner at Chicken Kitchen for less than $50. It makes sense to go ahead and apply. The worst that can happen is that the school says no.

Here's the other solution to the ubiquitous problem of obsessing about admissions to highly competitive colleges and universities. Focus on the abilities rather than the indicia thereof. Work on being the kid who should be accepted to an HSC rather than the kid who looks like she has the skills.

What can loving parents and decent counselors do to help?

Parents can help their kids avoid the road to nowhere by focusing on skills rather than on admissions. For elementary school kids, parents can read books to their kids rather than insist that the kids do the worksheets assigned for homework. And before you say, "Oh c'mon, David. Everybody knows that," let me repeat what hundreds of parents have told me: "By the time we have helped our kids with their homework, WE DON'T HAVE TIME TO READ TO THEM." Talk about irony. "Wake up, it's time for your sleeping pill." Hopefully, the point of homework is to help kids love learning. Worst-case scenario, the point of homework for little ones is to help them learn. Nah. The point of homework is about power and control. That homework is contraindicated for little ones is a subject for another book. (You might like my friend, Alfie Kohn's cogent *The Homework Myth: Why Our Kids Get Too Much of a Bad Thing.*) For now, think about it, what could possibly be the point of interminable, unpleasant worksheets other than to destroy a love of learning? What could compare to cuddling up with mom or dad on the couch and reading Winnie the Pooh? Especially when the research is so abundantly clear: For vocabulary acquisition, comprehension, and unadulterated joy, Edward Bear beats every homework worksheet ever created paws down.

For older kids, parents can—let me put this as politely as I can—shut the hell up. There is no reason to talk about admissions to HSCs. Ever. If the kids come to you with a question, by all means answer it. But if the parent begins For older kids, parents can—let me put this as politely as I can—shut the hell up. There is no reason to talk about admissions to HSCs. Ever. If the kids come to you with a question, by all means answer it. But if the parent begins the conversation, anxiety will likely lead down a rabbit hole from which there is no return.

"But all the parents in the parking lot at the high school are talking about where their kids are applying. As early as ninth grade. No one talks about anything else. It's all Harvard this and test prep that. Each and every time I go to pick up my kid, three parents ask me where my daughter is applying to college. The questions are endless. There are meetings at the school. There are reams of papers being sent home. There is an unrelenting spotlight focused on each child's rank in class and where the kids are applying and who got in where last year. It's getting to the point where I don't want to talk to anyone at the school."

Not talking to anyone might be a good place to start. (Unless of course they have also read and understood this book. In which case you might want to go have a nice cup of coffee and chat about something else.) It seems these parents have nothing else to talk about other than sharing their screaming anxiety about admissions to HSCs.

Think about it: No one would dare come into your home and ask you how much you paid for it. No one would dare ask you how often you and your partner made love last month. Yes these same people ask you where your child is applying to college as if your daughter were one of those ducks hanging upside down in the window of those restaurants in Chinatown. Where your child is applying to college is no one's business. Where your child is applying to college is a private family matter. Your family is not a reality show.

Here is a snarky response that will allow you to dissuade rubber-necking busy-bodies from asking you personal questions that are none of their concern about where your beloved child is applying to college:

Annoying Over Reaching Know-It-All: So, where is your daughter applying to college?

You: Are we married?

Annoying Over Reaching Know-It-All: No, of course not. You know my husband; he works downtown.

You: Then we'll have to talk about something less personal.

Of course sometimes these unbearable nosy boots go straight to your children. Here is an opportunity to stand up for your child and communicate that you love her for who she is not for where she applies to college.

Unpleasant Snooping Meddlesome Parent: So, Susie. Where are you applying to college?

Your Daughter: I would love to tell you but my mom is a privacy freak and she says if I tell anyone where I am applying then she won't let me go to college.

By not playing the game, you automatically win. No one can talk about you if you don't talk about yourself. No one can compare. No one can point a finger. And best of all, no one will know. If you have learned only one thing from this book, it is that who the child is matters more than where she goes to school. It is hurtful to your child if intrusive prying classmates and families have enough information to blather on in confidential whispers: "You know that Susie? She thinks she's so great. She took five APs and had 400 community service hours, but she got rejected from Dartmouth and waitlisted at Cornell."

Come April of senior year your daughter may very well be rejected at Dartmouth. (If you have learned only two things from this book, you know that there is a casino aspect to admissions.) If she is rejected at Dartmouth—and no one outside your nuclear family knows that— then the sting of rejection may last 20 minutes. If everyone in the high school and the community is gossiping about it, the misery of the bad roll of the dice can last for weeks.

YET ANOTHER EXAMPLE

A BUDDY OF MINE RECENTLY SOLD HIS medical practice. Of course, polite people—even close friends—don't talk about money, but my understanding is that Hillary obtained a significant number of samoleans. As well she should. Bright girl, worked hard, good doctor. But I did not write a book about social niceties. (Friends don't ask friends how much money they entered retirement with.) As my gentle leaders will doubtless have noticed by now, this book is about whether or not your child's choice of undergraduate institution determines her future.

So The question is: where did my buddy go to undergraduate college? Actually, she didn't.

She went to community college. Miami Dade Junior College, it was called in those days. After two years, she transferred to Florida Atlantic University. Again, hardly a household name. Then to medical school at the University of Miami. Followed by a successful career and retirement at a reasonable age.

How would her life have been different if she had gone to a "name" school? What advantages would she have found at a highly selective college?

She might have been graduated with more debt. She might not have been able to retire at such an early age.

She had the ability, the motivation, and the study skills get the job done. Where she went to college had nothing to do with her subsequent success.

Chapter 34

IN SUMMARY, AND WITHOUT HUMOR OR IRONY

1) ADMISSIONS TO HIGHLY SELECTIVE colleges is...

- hard on kids
- hard on families
- essentially random (beyond a point)

2) Lots of highly successful people attended no name colleges. Lots of unsuccessful people went to HSCs.

3) It's the kid in the college, not the college in the kid.

4) Your child and your family will be better served by focusing on that which will be more beneficial—learning—rather than obsessing on admission to HSCs.

5) The reality of ability not the indicators of ability will help your child. Think knowledge over grades.

6) College admissions will take care of itself. An able student will be fine, whether or not she is admitted to an HSC.

7) Embracing your family's privacy is a step toward mental health and a strong family.

BIBLIOGRAPHY

Altshuler, David, *Kids Learn What they Live. Kids Live What They Learn*, Langley Press, 2016.

Altshuler, David, *Love the Kid You Get. Get the Kid You Love*, Langley Press, 2014.

Altshuler, David, *Raising Healthy Kids in an Unhealthy World*, Langley Press, 2013.

Antonoff, Steven R., *The College Finder: Choose the School That's Right for You*, Wintergreen Orchard House, 2017.

Berman, Susan, *The Underground Guide to the College of Your Choice: The only Handbook that Tells You What's Really Happening at Every Major College and University in the U.S.A.*, 1971, Signet.

Bruni, Frank, *Where You Go Is Not Who You'll Be: An Antidote to the College Admissions Mania*, 2015, Hachette Book Group, Inc.

Hirsh-Pasek and Golinkoff, Roberta Michnick, *Einstein Never Used Flash Cards: How Our Children REALLY Learn—and Why They Need to Play More and Memorize Less,* 2003, Rodale.

Israel, Jerry, *The 75 Biggest Myths about College Admissions: Stand Out from the Pack, Avoid Mistakes, and Get Into the College of Your Dreams*, 2008, Sourcebooks, Inc.

Kohn, Alfie, *What to Look for in a Classroom … and Other Essays*, 1998, Jossey-Bass.

Marie, Rosalind P. Marie and Law, Claire, *Find the Perfect College for You: 82 Exceptional Schools that Fit your Personality and Learning Style*, SuperCollege LLC, 2012.

Moll, Richard, *Playing the Private College Admissions Game: The Indispensable Insider's Guide to Getting into the Most Selective Schools*, 1986, Penguin Books.

Orr, Tamra B., *America's Best Colleges for B Students: A College Guide for Students without Straight A's*, second edition, SuperCollege, LLC, 2007.

Pipher, Mary, Ph.D., *Reviving Ophelia: Saving the Selves of Adolescent Girls*, Putnam Books, 1994.

Pope, Loren, revised by Hilary Masell Oswald, *Colleges that Change Lives: 40 Schools That Will Change The Way You Think About College*, 4th edition, 2016, Penguin Books.

Springer, Sally P., Reider, Jon, and Vining Morgan, Joyce, *Admissions Matters: What Students And Parents Need To Know About Getting Into College*, 2013, Jossey-Bass.

Sykes, Charles and Miner, Brad, *The National Review College Guide: America's Top Liberal Arts Schools*, 1993, Simon and Schuster.

NOTES

Made in the USA
Columbia, SC
07 November 2017